THE BEAUTY DEFENSE

TRUE CRIME HISTORY

THE BEAUTY DEFENSE

Femmes Fatales on Trial

LAURA JAMES

The Kent State University Press

KENT, OHIO

ISBN 978-1-60635-394-3
Manufactured in the United States of America

Cataloging information for this title is available at the Library of Congress.

24 23 22 21 20   5 4 3 2 1

FOR JOE, *for everything*

CONTENTS

INTRODUCTION

The Femme Fatale

According to an ages-old *lex non scripta,* beauty alone is an affirmative defense to any criminal charge, even premeditated murder.[1] A seductive woman who is aware of her privilege is dangerous to her lovers. We know her kind from legend, the Bible, fiction, true crime, and film. For four hundred years, we have called her a femme fatale.[2]

Some of the ancients believed that beautiful women are venomous, and early stories of the femmes fatales who live and kill among us describe them as literally poisonous. The Greek philosopher Socrates is said to have warned that a beauty's kiss was deadlier than a spider's venom. "What do you think you would suffer after kissing someone beautiful? Would you not immediately be a slave rather than free?" asked Socrates. "I counsel you . . . whenever you see someone beautiful, to flee without looking back."[3]

Classical literature is filled with infectious damsels and dead heroes. "The betrayal of a king or hero by his mistress is, in short, a story both old and popular," writes historian Wolfgang Lederer, "and many a man has actually lost his life because of it: from Samson who lost his hair and hide through Delilah, to the various victims of Mata Hari and her successors of today. . . . The 'demon woman' is a mythological type, and appears either as the companion of the enemy, or as the seductress of the hero; she sleeps with him—or at least promises to—and kills him."[4] The old tales always depicted the femme fatale as a grown woman, not a girl. "Since the World began, Lilith has been a mature woman," observed an aesthete. "In history and literature the Dangerous Woman was always the Older Woman."[5]

Among the faded legends from that ancient time are the stories of immortals who were beautiful and terrible and who were specifically infamous for slaughtering men. They were Medusa, a great beauty before a curse made her visage fatal to men; Circe, who lived in a cave and turned men into swine; the Sirens, whose promising calls led sailors to shipwreck; the Irish goddess Anu, who lived in a cave and ate men alive; Scylla, the six-headed bitch who lived in a cave and ate sailors alive; Lilith, the night demon with a ravenous appetite for men; Kali, the Hindu goddess and slayer of men; and even Aphrodite, otherwise known as Venus. It is easy to forget that the ancient goddess of love and sex also commanded every woman on the island of Lemnos to murder her husband. According to the old stories, they obeyed her command.[6] *Cave amantem* was the saying of the ancients—*of her love, beware.*

The Bible also regales us with accounts of toxic beauties, from Eve who tempted Adam to the alluring descendants of Eve. Judith, a beauti-

Samson and Delilah by Peter Paul Rubens (1609). (Public domain, via Wikimedia Commons.)

ful widow, adorned herself with ribbons, rich perfumes, and fine jewels to seduce the enemy's general Holofernes, and then she beheaded him with his own sword. Delilah bewitched and then betrayed her lover Samson to the Philistines for twelve hundred pieces of silver, becoming a wealthy woman. Salome danced for Herod and demanded the head of John the Baptist, murdering by proxy with sex appeal alone. They have served ever since as synonyms for fatally seductive women and as the muses of innumerable artists, immortalized in oil by the likes of Caravaggio, Klimt, Rubens, and so many others drawn to the junction of beauty and bloodshed.

As wicked and fascinating as these legendary women have always been, the most frightening examples of the "fairer sex" are to be found not in old stories but in the case law. Our collective legal history teems with larger-than-life women who committed outrageous acts and whose good looks are the only explanation for the illogical outcomes of their cases.

CITY OF ATHENS VS. PHRYNE (336 BC)

First Recorded Instance of a Successful Beauty Defense

Modern historians assure us this old trial report is probably true. In Athens, Greece, twenty-four hundred years ago, Phryne, thirty-five, a famous *courtisane,* which we can generously translate as a woman of many lovers, was charged with impiety and put on trial. The mandatory penalty was death. The case went badly for Phryne. When it became apparent that she may lose her life, her attorney Hypereides, who was also one of her many lovers, took desperate measures. She had no other defense. He pulled off her robe under which she wore nothing and showed the judges her beauty bare. Silently pleading on behalf of all mankind, he studied the reaction of the officials to the sight of Phryne's body. Moved by her, undoubtedly experiencing *émotions complexes,* officially moved by pity, the judges acquitted the lovely defendant.

The legend of Phryne's physical form survives today in oil and marble. Botticelli and many others have painted her, and she was rumored to be the inspiration for the most famous sculpture of Aphrodite, goddess of love (and, lest we forget, goddess of husband-slaughtering). In more literate times, her name was a euphemism for nudity; one could be said to

Oedipus and the Sphinx by Gustave Moreau (1864). (Public domain, via Creative Commons.)

appear "as Phryne before the elders."[7] In criminal history, she serves as a symbol of that barest of defenses—feminine attractiveness.

Thousands of years later, a lawyer in France rested a light hand on the shoulder of a certain American stunner to be named later. Turning to the men in the jury box, he declared, "Elle est trop belle pour tre mauvais" (she is too beautiful to be bad). He did not have to disrobe her to make his point. The jury indeed acquitted her of fatally shooting her husband.

The sordid story of a lovely woman, a weapon, a dead man, and an acquittal has played itself out in courtrooms across the globe, on front pages around the world, for generations. Regardless of evidence, burdens of proof, and jury instructions in a supposedly dispassionate court of law, justice is not blind to beauty. Even in a trial concerning the cold-blooded, premeditated murder of another human being, it is the defendant's looks, good or bad, that are judged first. If she is pretty, jurors will hear her out and even want to believe her; if she is ugly, they will hear both sides. The law may not reach even the obviously guilty murderess if she meets the requirements to be gleaned from the case studies of those lethal ladies who have committed unpunished crimes. To get away with murder, a woman need only follow the common law—five established if unwritten rules of feminine misconduct:[8]

1. She must be beautiful.
2. She must kill a lover.
3. She must act alone.
4. She must kill only once.
5. She must have a good attorney.

RULE 1: SHE MUST BE BEAUTIFUL

Prolific true crime historian Jay Robert Nash once observed, "Most female criminals are unattractive, many of them even physically repulsive." Nash was particularly repulsed by the visage of Belle Starr, describing the outlaw queen as a "hatchet-faced harridan with a maniacal stare." He was not wrong, but it is also true that in order for a woman to become a convicted criminal in the first place, she could not be very attractive. If Belle Starr had been beautiful, she never would have made her way into Nash's encyclopedia of female convicts.[9]

Beautiful women are above the law. Women on trial for serious crimes do not need defenses. They need jailhouse makeovers. Curlers, dresses, and lipstick. Every defendant gives "demeanor evidence" for the court, whether she testifies or not. A pretty face will make its statement without saying a word. Good bones have jury appeal. What man can punish a delicate flower of femininity?

The woman on trial must of course dress carefully for the occasion. Beulah May Annan's attorneys hired a "fashion expert" to help with her trial appearance.[10] They decided on the most popular and well-received costume for an accused murderess, which has long been a tailored black dress with a hemline at least below the knee and touches of white at the collar and cuffs. We may add, en passant, that a sufficiently high social class or great wealth might make up to a degree for lack of attractiveness, since money has the effect of improving one's appearance. The same is true for crying. A feminine, well-timed fainting spell only underscores her point. As a psychology professor observed in 1915, "It is perfectly natural and normal for the masculine mind in a jury box to react tremendously to feminine tears and distress. Try as the intellect may to steel the judgment against such an appeal, it usually fails to a marked degree."[11]

There are unconscious presumptions at work when a woman is accused of a grave crime. It is not easy for some jurors to accept the fact that men do not have a monopoly on murder and they never have. One presumption is that a pretty woman is incapable of criminal behavior, while an ugly woman has no defense to the facts. Beautiful women have always been less likely to get convicted. Historically, a defendant who was not particularly pretty could still be rendered sufficiently girlish for the law to take it easy on her. As one scandalized representative of the people declared in 1912, "The defendant need not be beautiful; if she merely appears feminine on the stand she is safe."[12] Added a prosecutor who tried to secure a murder conviction against one Cora Orthwein for blasting her boyfriend into the afterlife: "It's the same old story. You can't convict a woman if she is good looking." Hilda Exlund might have gotten away with stabbing her husband to death, except that she was a forty-five-year-old Swedish immigrant with a powerful physique, and she was not attractive. After she was convicted in 1919, Hilda exclaimed, "I suppose if I had been young and beautiful, I would have been turned loose just as other women who have been tried for killing their husbands."[13]

The best strategy for an ugly woman accused of murder is to blame her bad looks on the victim. Mary Colucci killed her husband Joe on a New York train. She was not pretty enough to arouse that certain sort of sympathy with male jurors, not with jagged teeth and a crooked nose. So her lawyer, the legendary Samuel S. Leibowitz, put her on the stand and asked her, "How many times did your husband break your nose?"

"Fifteen times," she answered.

"Step down and let the jury look at your nose."

Later in his closing argument Leibowitz said, "After viewing that nose, can there be any doubt as to what kind of beast her husband was? Can there be any doubt that she had a right to protect herself?"

The jury let her go.[14]

RULE 2: SHE MUST KILL A LOVER

They are by definition femmes fatales. Sometimes the term is misapplied to ladies who only ruin men financially, like the beautiful *horizontale* Cora Pearl[15] and women who did not actually kill their victims. A true femme fatale is lethal. But for the fact that she was a bad shot and only wounded her lover, Alice de Janzé probably would have earned a place in this compilation.[16] Likewise, Zeo Zoe Wilkins[17] and Marie Bière[18] were beautiful monsters who couldn't hit the broad side of a man.

For every murderess, there must be one unfortunate murderee. It is husbands and lovers who are not safe in the embrace of a *belle dame sans merci.*[19] Next to a pretty face, a man's very life may be and has been shrugged off, not worth equal consideration, *if* he partook of the poisoned dish—or in some cases merely *tried* to, according only to her. This is true in part because "the public has shown, unmistakably, that most of all it likes to read about murders which are motivated by sex in one form or another."[20]

However, the death of a stranger at the hands of a femme fatale may well shock the public conscience. She risks genuine punishment. As a consequence of this provision of the *lex non scripta,* even an extraordinarily beautiful woman might not get away with murdering someone she does not know. Toni Jo Henry, who shot and killed a stranger who gave her a ride, learned this the hard way. The state of Louisiana electrocuted her in 1942, smoldering eyes and all, making her arguably the most beautiful American ever put to death.[21] Her rival for the distinction is Barbara Graham, who was certainly lovely enough to get away with almost anything—except killing an elderly woman for her cash. Courtroom hysterics are not always effective; Barbara died in the gas chamber.[22]

Blond-haired, blue-eyed Penny Bjorkland stunned California in 1959 when she shot a stranger at random and airily told police that she did it

Cora Pearl, often mistakenly dubbed a *femme fatale,* was the most glamorous and daring of the nineteenth-century Parisian demi-mondaines. She never shot any of her lovers, though one shot himself on her doorstep. (Public domain, via Wikimedia Commons.)

because she felt like murdering somebody. "I just woke up one morning and decided, today would be the day," she later confessed. "Today would be the day I would finally kill someone." The unfortunate "someone" was a young husband and father named August Norry. Though Penny was young and pretty, she served seven years.[23] Clara Phillips of Los Angeles was also good-looking enough to get away with murder, but not the killing of another woman, and not with a hammer. The lady who came to be known as "Tiger Girl" had to serve more than thirteen years.

Katherine "Kitty" Malm was only nineteen years old when she committed a robbery with her husband Otto Malm, who killed a security guard. She was certain she was going to be acquitted. "Hang me?" she asked. "That's a joke. Say, nobody in the world would hang a girl for bein' in an alley with a guy who pulls a gun and shoots." The jurors knew the rules for murderesses better than Kitty Malm. She was so surprised when they convicted her, she fainted. She went to Joliet Prison in tears. As one reporter observed, "her mistake was in being 'hard boiled' and none too good looking."[24]

A Bonnie Parker type may be able to participate in a mass murder and still be acquitted but only if she is very attractive, dresses carefully, and can cry on cue. Pretty Peggy Paulos and her boyfriend Leo Hall lit up the night of March 28, 1934, in Kitsap County, Washington, slaughtering six men in a botched robbery. At her trial, the twenty-seven-year-old defendant wore tight ringlets all over her head and a cotton Sunday dress. She looked half her age and sobbed throughout the proceedings. Her boyfriend got the rope. She was cleared of all charges.

Chicago's Wanda Stopa, a beautiful young lawyer with crazy blue eyes, bulldozed her way into her lover's home, where she confronted her lover's wife and then shot and killed his caretaker, Henry Manning. After the murder Wanda went mad and fled to Detroit, where she died just like murderess Lady Macbeth, offstage and by her own hand. Wanda took a fatal dose of cyanide. As an attorney, she would have known she might not get away with shooting a bystander.

Similarly, Adrienne Eckhardt of Vienna was pretty enough to get away with murder—if only she hadn't beaten the poor man to death with a meat grinder mere hours after meeting him in a pub. The best trial attorney in Austria could not save her on those facts. She had to serve more than a decade in prison.

An angel-faced teenager once committed a savage double murder of people who were strangers to her. Thankfully, Texas frowns on disembowelment in every instance. Karla Faye Tucker made herself notorious for a vulgar bloodbath, and yet just before her well-deserved execution, she was the object of an extraordinary effort to save her life. Her gorgeous face was on the TV news regularly for weeks as she touted her jailhouse religious conversion as grounds for mercy to Texas governor George W. Bush. Those journalists who favored pretty Karla Faye with airtime knew when they were doing it that it was her good looks and not the abjectly awful facts of her case that garnered her the attention that came close to saving her from the consequences of her repulsive conduct. As reporter Bob Harris quipped, "The only reason anyone gave a ding-dang about this woman was because she was really cute, which gave the TV cameras something to point at."[25] Texas executed Karla Faye Tucker anyway. Governor Bush released a statement explaining why he refused to commute Miss Tucker's sentence: "When I was sworn in as the governor of Texas I took an oath of office to uphold the laws of our state, including the death penalty. My responsibility is to ensure our laws are enforced fairly and evenly without preference or special treatment. . . . Karla Faye Tucker has acknowledged she is guilty of a horrible crime. . . . She was convicted and sentenced by a jury of her peers. The role of the state is to enforce our laws and to make sure all individuals are treated fairly under those laws. . . . May God bless Karla Faye Tucker and may God bless her victims and their families." The Beauty Defense almost saved this butcher, but she broke too many rules.

Her story is one example of the power of the press to influence the process in a pretty woman's favor. Reporters have always loved a good, juicy story, even if they have to shoehorn a bad story into the good story's narrative because good stories sell newspapers. One can understand if not forgive the journalistic tendency to edit out facts that do not fit the headline, to say nothing of the photo caption. As a prestigious journalism professor has observed, "Since the advent of the penny press nearly two centuries ago, American journalists have done some of their briskest business when selling tales of unlikely female perpetrators—the more frail and photogenic, the better."[26]

RULE 3: SHE MUST ACT ALONE

A femme fatale is asking for punishment if she kills her lover with the help of another lover. Among the well-known women who made this often-fatal error are Marie Manning, Alice Arden,[27] Katharine Nairn,[28] Bathsheba Spooner,[29] Ruth Snyder,[30] Ann Bilansky,[31] Ada LeBoeuf,[32] Edith Thompson,[33] and countless lesser-known women, such as Madame Lescombat and Grete Beier. Hiring thugs for the job landed Anna Antonio of New York in the electric chair in 1934.[34]

Women throughout hundreds of years of history and across the world who otherwise might have qualified for consideration in this compilation instead made the singular error of taking aid from a lover, thereby proving not only premeditation but an indecent motive. This type of case is truly frightening to the average man, perhaps because it happens so randomly and can take a poor fellow entirely by surprise.

Then there is the exception that proves the rule. If a villainess is going to have a lover, she should get them wholesale—never stop at just one. A femme fatale who has two lovers kill a third, or three lovers kill a fourth, will go free, if the stories that follow are any indication; how-

Frances Howard Carr, Countess of Somerset, was convicted of the murder by mercuric chloride of Sir Thomas Overbury but was pardoned by King James I. (Wikimedia Commons.)

ever, based on the case law, it seems one must be born a countess to fall within this exception.

A countess is by long extralegal tradition free to write her own laws. This has been true since at least the sixteenth century, when the Blood Countess, Elizabeth Bathory, sadistically tortured and slaughtered dozens if not hundreds of young women from 1585 to 1609. Countess Dracula managed to avoid trial and was allowed to die a natural death.[35] Another countess who received preferential treatment was Frances Howard Carr, Countess of Somerset. It is the world's great loss that newspapers had yet to be invented[36] in 1613, when the countess was the defendant in one of the biggest murder trials in the history of high society.[37] The countess confessed to poisoning the poet Sir Thomas Overbury and was found guilty of his murder. Yet she was pardoned by the king. Her portrait and title explain it all.[38]

RULE 4: SHE MUST KILL ONLY ONCE

A lovely woman may be free to kill, but she had better not do it again. Serial murder is a risky business even for a beauty. Many a femme fatale has garnered an acquittal and then pushed her luck. The criminal records of womankind are replete with warning examples of women who took things one homicide too far and were then imprisoned or worse.

Society playgirl Evelyn Dick was lovely enough to elude a murder rap for the death of her husband John in one of the most spectacular trials in Canadian history, but she could not beat a child murder charge.[39] Louise Peete got away with shooting down Joe Appel, but she was later convicted of murdering Jacob Denton in Los Angeles.[40] Sharon Kinne might have gotten away with her husband's murder if she could have ended it there, and if she hadn't bragged, "I've shot men before and managed to get out of it."[41] Another woman who pressed her luck was Hazel Glab, the eternal regret of John Glab. She might have walked after shooting her husband if she hadn't later tried to defraud the estate of her wealthy fiancé. Josephine Gray's husband was murdered by a gunshot to the head. Two witnesses told police she had tried to hire them to murder him. She threatened those witnesses with voodoo, flashed a winning smile in her arrest photos, eluded any type of sanction, and collected a handsome life insurance settlement. But when she killed two more men whose lives were insured in her favor, she upset the adjusters. They pursued the matter. She went to prison—not for murder but for insurance fraud.[42]

RULE 5: SHE MUST HAVE A GOOD ATTORNEY

It should go without saying that a femme fatale needs a champion for the forensic battle, a powerful lawyer to play Hypereides to her Phryne. More than a good argument, a damsel in legal distress needs good legal advice. Guided by a lawyer who understands the niceties of the unwritten laws, a guilty woman with special help can make a joke of any legislative pronouncements. The very best of the defense bar are drawn to attractive killers, enticed by the prospect of a dramatic acquittal and all the glory to come from putting a confessed killer back on the streets to pose a further pretty threat to mankind. Of course the attorney is best served by keeping her at a healthy emotional distance as so many have fallen in love with dangerous female clients. During the murder inquest regarding Countess Tarnovska, it was a prosecutor who ruined himself with his infatuation for her, and he wasn't the first lawyer to fall madly in love with the countess. Something similar happened in the case of femme fatale Madalynne

Obenchain. It has probably happened to countless other prosecutors and defense attorneys who could hide it better than they could.[43]

Many of the learned counselors mentioned in this book were at the heights of their mesmeric powers when retained to play the devil's advocate for a femme fatale. Some of their deviling for these witches has been reprinted and lauded by other lawyers for generations. The cross-examinations of Sir Edward Clarke for Adelaide Bartlett, the argument of Samuel Leibowitz for Vera Stretz, the Dickens speech for Kitty Byron, and the dramatics of Marshall Hall for Madame Fahmy are among the storied trial performances to come. "Lawyers wield an hypnotic influence over the average jury," as we have long known, "and women are encouraged to take a chance on murder when they recall the long list of trials in which women were acquitted on the strength of their lawyers' impassioned pleas."[44]

Some women have learned the hard way that a lousy lawyer can send a would-be femme fatale straight to prison for a long stretch of time. Mattie Howard, once known to law enforcement in Kansas City as "Agate Eyes," or "Queen of the Underworld," might have earned a place in this roundup had she hired a better attorney to handle her front-page murder trial in 1918. But she hired the son of Jesse James to represent her. The Junior James, the worst attorney in the history of Missouri, instructed this beauty to eat nuts and grapes during the prosecution's case, she said, "so as to appear nonchalant." That was a terrible blunder on her part. She should have wept, fainted, or both. The jury convicted her in no small part because of her lousy demeanor evidence. Mattie blamed Jesse James Junior, and she was certainly right when she lamented her choice of counsel. When it came time for her lawyer to file an appeal brief on her behalf, her hopes must have soared. As a woman, she stood an excellent chance on appeal of getting a new trial, maybe even winning her release. But her lousy lawyer did not even bother to file a brief on her behalf. He let his client go to prison and stay there. Poor Mattie had to give up her plan to turn her infamy into a Hollywood career. She actually had to serve several years for the murder she helped commit.[45]

Perhaps surprisingly, it does not matter *where* a femme fatale decides to kill her lover. The setting for a murder can be in full public view for all it seems to matter in the case of an attractive woman. A jilted lady named Mary Harris murdered her former lover Adoniram J. Burroughs in broad daylight on the steps of the US Treasury building in Washington, DC, on January 30, 1865. Mrs. Lincoln sent her flowers in jail. She pleaded temporary insanity and was acquitted.[46]

Ironically, many similar murders have happened *inside* courthouses. Another interesting law never found in published statutes once applied to any woman who was pregnant and jilted. The Honor Exception allowed such a woman to murder her lover to avenge her honor and escape sanction by the state, whether pretty (like Lastencia Abarta and Clara Fallmer of California, or Texan Winnie Morris) or lacking in feminine charms. On February 2, 1909, the expecting and jilted Vera Ware, who was "not altogether unattractive, but she would not be classified as a beauty," murdered her former lover John Hanes inside the picturesque Coryell County Courthouse in Gatesville, Texas. While many saw this hideous premeditated murder as an inexcusable insult to the rule of law—committed no less within the walls of the House of the Law, flouting every principle and commandment that the judicial pillar of the community stood for—a jury acquitted her of the crime.[47]

Likewise, Emma Simpson shot her husband in a courtroom in Chicago in 1919. "You've killed him!" the court reporter yelled. She replied, "I hope so!" Then she said, "I will need no attorney—the new unwritten law will save me. I will tell my whole story to the jury and they will free me."[48] Indeed they did.

Collectively, the stories that follow are a warning to men everywhere to never buy your gal a .32. It is a small gun that easily fits the palm of a small hand, and five of the femmes fatales featured in this book used a .32 to commit their crimes. Generally speaking, however, it really does not seem to matter one whit which method a handsome woman chooses for ending the life of a man who is inconvenient to her, as you will see.

Virtually all of the ladies who follow acted more or less in compliance with all five of the rules for murderesses, and they almost all got away scot-free. Once in a while, however, in a surprising twist, the law refuses to make a complete ass of itself when there's a beauty in the dock.

BEULAH ANNAN

THE VICTIMS: At least 320 men, including Harry Kalstedt
WHEN: From 1875 to 1925; for Kalstedt, April 23, 1924
WHERE: Chicago, Illinois
DEFENSE COUNSEL: William Scott Stewart

THE CASE

Well into the 1700s, in the Western world, a black widow was punished with strangulation—then for good measure she was burned to ashes at the stake. Much later, in a booming city in the midwestern United States, there was no sanction whatsoever for the ultimate domestic rebellion.

For decades, conditions were perfect in Chicago for a raging murder epidemic. The city was awash in guns and cheap booze, and something unthinkable happened. *Mariticide,* the killing of one's husband, was *en vogue.* Chicago's homicidal wives feared no punishment beyond making it onto page one for a week or two, or until the next celebrated mariticide. Otherwise, once the lout was dead, their problems were solved and they could go about their lives unmolested by the law.

For entire generations, women killers were hardly ever punished if they followed the rules and simply killed, *unaided,* a husband or a boyfriend. Self-made widows got off in Chicago "unless the homicide was particularly grisly or the killer challenged established social mores."[1] The all-time acquittal rate for female killers hovered around the 90 percent mark. Absent unusual facts, any sufficiently feminine woman committing a sufficiently feminine "love crime" could not be convicted of murder in Cook County, Illinois.

Beulah Annan and Al Annan sitting with William Scott Stewart. (DN-0076803, *Chicago Daily News* negatives collection, Chicago History Museum.)

In many cases, the murderous wife claimed that the homicide followed years of physical abuse. The police were not always impressed. If a woman can shoot a man for hitting her, the police theorized, Chicago would soon be short of husbands.

Mary Camilla told police she had to kill Joseph Camilla because he was drunk and threatening her life. Mary Frank killed Mr. Frank for the same reason. Lena Musso said her husband came after her with a razor, so she had to shoot him. Who could say otherwise? Rosie Guszck killed her husband with a knife—"I was unable to stand his abuse any longer." Grace Doyle committed an act of "self-defense in advance" to stop the beatings. Iva Barnes shot her abusive husband dead on a sidewalk. Annie Olsen shot her sleeping husband August after years of death threats from him, she said. Minnie Smith said she was beaten for years: "He always said if I ever had him arrested he would kill me, and I know he would do it. So I shot him—and then I shot him some more."

Most of these mariticides were clearly premeditated. Mary Wiley pawned a skirt to buy a gun to shoot her husband. Jessie Hopkins borrowed a gun from her father. Mary Shea hid a gun under her bed. Iva

Beulah Annan poses for the press in her jail cell. (DN-0076797, *Chicago Daily News* negatives collection, Chicago History Museum.)

Barnes asked Mr. Barnes to wait for her on the street while she got her gun, then shot him twice; he fell, and she shot him twice more. One woman carried an article in her purse describing the acquittals of fourteen husband-killers. She brought that article with her when she shot her husband.[2] Murder begat murder begat murder and so on for decades. In April 1918, Ruby Dean became the twenty-fifth woman to be acquitted in a decade. Her frustrated prosecutor declared husband-murder to be "the king"—perhaps he meant the *queen*—"of indoor sports."[3]

At one point, thirty-five consecutive women were acquitted in the Cook County Courthouse of killing their husbands. As defense attorney Helen Cirese explained it, "Have you ever seen the look of hopeless anxiety, of utter misery upon the face of an accused prisoner? Have you, then, seen the looks on that same face when twelve solemn men slowly file in and inform the court their verdict is 'Not Guilty'? The mingled joy, the relief, the moist eyes, the trembling lips, the simple words of thanks—that is truly romance—the romance of law."

In this romantic environment, the femmes fatales flourished.

Beulah Annan is widely considered the most beautiful of all the Chicago man-killers, even the prettiest woman ever accused of murder in

Belva Gaertner sits with her attorney, Thomas D. Nash. (DN-0077649, *Chicago Daily News* negatives collection, Chicago History Museum.)

Chicago. She was arrested anyway because some thought Venus deserved a noose even if everything she said about murdering her lover was true. The papers would call her "a modern Salome." Then again, she said some pretty astonishing things about killing poor Harry, such as, "He knew I was going to quit him and words led to words." Words, apparently, were motive enough. She never did say what Harry called her that sent her running for a gun. "He said he was through with me and began to put on his coat. When I saw that he meant what he said, my mind went in a whirl, and I shot him.

"We both ran to the bedroom, where a revolver was kept. I got there first. They say I shot him in the back, but it must have been sort of under the arm."

After she shot him—in the back, actually—she put on a phonograph recording of a fox-trot called "Hula Lou." "Her name was Hula Lou / The kinda gal that never could be true / She did her dancin' in the evenin' breeze / 'Neath the trees."[4] She played the song over and over and over again on her Victrola while Harry Kalstedt bled out on the floor. Her husband Al came home to find a dead man in his bedroom. It would fall to poor Al to clean up all the blood.

The victim had met Mrs. Annan only two months before she killed him. He had walked into a Chicago laundry where the redheaded beauty fresh from Kentucky worked. Perhaps he never learned she was a woman who avidly followed murderesses in the newspapers.

Beulah Annan's heroine was a man-killer named Belva "Belle" Gaertner, thirty-eight, who shot her lover of three months, Walter Law, a twenty-nine-year-old married car salesman, on March 12, 1924, and left him for dead in her car. Later that morning, police showed up at Belle's front door to ask her about the man they found in her Nash sedan with a bullet hole in his head. "I don't know," she told them. "I was drunk." She admitted they had been fighting. "We got drunk and he got killed—I don't know how." She would later add that they were arguing over who was the better shot. At an inquest into the death of Walter Law, a colleague of the dead man testified that the victim was afraid of Belva Gaertner and had even considered buying more life insurance, convinced that his mistress was planning to kill him. Further evidence showed that he was trying to break off with her. For her part, Belva Gaertner literally played off his death like it was all just a game. "I suggested, jokingly, that we toss up a coin and that the winner shoot the loser. I said if the winner missed, the loser would get a chance to shoot, and vice versa, until one of us was shot. There were nine bullets in the pistol. And then—oh, I don't know just what did happen. I was too drunk. . . . I remember seeing him collapse over the wheel, but I had no idea what was the matter." So was born the "Flip-Coin Murderess." She enjoyed the attention and gave innumerable interviews from her jail cell. Said Belva, "That coroner's jury that held me for murder—that was bum. They were narrow-minded old birds— bet they never heard a jazz band in their lives. Now, if I'm tried, I want worldly men, broad-minded men, men who know what it is to get out a bit. Why, no one like that would convict me." She was right. Belva Gaertner was acquitted by a jury. She posed for pictures with jurors while her victim's widow, Freda Law, cried out, "Walter paid—why shouldn't she?"

Beulah Annan knew all about Belle Gaertner and even clipped articles from the papers about the nonchalant killer. Beulah learned from reading the papers that Chicago was the safest place of all for a woman to kill a man for no good reason whatsoever, other than to get her picture on the front page. Posing for photos was one thing Beulah did well. The roses and love letters began arriving at her jail cell within a day of her arrest for killing Harry Kalstedt, and Beulah Annan had her picture taken in jail with Belle Gaertner.

Beulah got a show trial. The prosecutor pleaded with the all-male jury on behalf of the remaining men of the city. "You must decide whether you want to let another pretty woman go out and say 'I got away with it!'"

Beulah Annan's posttrial separation from her husband put her in the headlines all over again. (From the *Wichita Daily Times*, Wichita Falls, Texas, July 26, 1924. Public domain, via Newspaperarchive.com.)

Detailed, illustrated stories of "Chicago's most beautiful slayer" were widely circulated for years. (From the *Hamilton [Ohio] Evening Journal*, May 5, 1928, via Newspaperarchive.com.)

She did get away with it. Said the prosecutor, "Another pretty woman gone free!"[5]

After her acquittal, Mrs. Annan declared she would be a devoted wife and forget all about the homicide she committed. She let the press know how remorseful she was. "Sorry? Who wouldn't be? But what is there to do? We can all be sorry after it's done. If only we could go back. If only we could! It's so little we get out of cheating. But the pleasure looks big, for the moment, doesn't it?" By Monday, she had split from Mr. Annan and hired a divorce lawyer. "I'm not going to waste the rest of my life with him—he's too slow." Instead, she would move to Hollywood and become an actress. Like many femmes fatales before and since, she made the mistake of thinking her instant immortality would translate to the silver screen.

The public would indeed clamor to hear her story. Unfortunately for Beulah, the American public preferred its causes célèbres to be veiled with a gauze of fiction, maybe to excuse their laughter. Beulah Annan lost her place in history to her fictional twin. It so happened that one of the reporters who covered Chicago's mariticide epidemic during the 1920s went on to write a satirical play in 1927 about the town's femmes fatales. Maurine Watkins's satire became the longest-running American musical in the history of Broadway, and it was eventually turned into an Oscar-winning film.

The playwright said she had intended to lampoon the quixotic American habit of turning killers into antiheroines and sentimentalizing cold-blooded murders. She used killer Belva Gaertner as the basis for the character "Velma Kelly," and Beulah Annan became "Roxie Hart." The author believed her play was "calling attention to evil." It may well have had some influence, for the streak of acquittals came to a halt around that time.

Regardless, more than three hundred men were murdered in this epidemic, and their graves became a backdrop for song and dance. The real Beulah Annan died of tuberculosis in 1928. But her fictional representation lives on in *Chicago: The Musical.*

ELVIRA BARNEY

> The psychopath is a rebel, a religious disobeyer of prevailing
> codes and standards . . . a rebel without a cause, an agitator
> without a slogan, a revolutionary without a program. . . .
> Psychopaths sparkle with the glitter of personal freedom, the
> checks and reins of the community are absent, and there are no
> limits either in a physical or a psychological sense.
> —Robert Lindner, *Rebel without a Cause*

THE VICTIM: Michael Scott Stephen
WHEN: May 31, 1932
WHERE: London, England
DEFENSE COUNSEL: Sir Patrick Hastings

THE CASE

Elvira Mullens was born with every advantage in life, including a slender figure, curly blond hair, and large gray eyes. Her father was a British knight, Sir John Mullens, her mother Lady Mullens. Her family had a house in Belgrave Square and a country seat in Sussex. She was evidently spoiled, for she made a disastrous decision early in life that set the tone for what was to come.

Elvira's first huge mistake was falling in love at first sight—in a dance hall. In a flight of fancy, she married an American cabaret singer and became Mrs. Barney. Months of dramatics ended in catastrophe when he left her with nothing but his name and returned to the United States. She had no way to serve him with a divorce. At a tender age, she was a deserted woman.

Thereafter Elvira lived the life of an untamed divorcée with unlimited funds. She took a place of her own near Knightsbridge, London, and her descent into degeneracy began. She was part of a pretentious set they called the "Bright Young Things."[1] For years she filled her nights with cliques of rich young people who frequented nightclubs and scandalized their neighbors.[2]

Cupid's next choice for Elvira Barney was Michael Stephen. Her lover was a banker's son who made his living attending cocktail parties. He gave his employment as "dress designer." He was exactly her age, from her social stratum, enjoyed drinking too much, and he, too, had fallen from grace. His well-to-do parents had cut off his allowance. Elvira and Michael were together for a year when their relationship took a bad turn. Elvira would admit they began to quarrel "from time to time." She would admit they fought over another woman he was fond of.

She would also admit hosting a party on May 30, 1932, at her place, inviting her usual set. Michael was in attendance. After the party they went to bed together, but they got in an argument. He left her bed and got dressed. Elvira would later claim Michael knew she kept a revolver. He did not know that she hid it from time to time. She claimed he knew she had started keeping it under the cushion of a chair near her bed. Her story continued:

"He took it, saying, 'I am going to take it away for fear you kill yourself.' He went into the room on the left. I ran after him and tried to get it back. . . . As we were struggling together—he wanted to take it away, and I wanted to get it back—it went off. Our hands were together—his hands and mine." He took a bullet to the chest and collapsed.

She called for a doctor, saying there had been an accident. When the doctor arrived, Michael was dead next to a hot gun and Elvira was beside herself. The doctor said he would call the police. Elvira objected and grew more hysterical. When the police arrived, her behavior was frenzied. She called them "vile swine" and ordered them to leave her home. She screamed and cried. When a police officer used her telephone, she grabbed it from his hands. When an officer said she would have to go to the police station for further questioning, she slapped him across the face.

Elvira was hauled downtown in a state of exhaustion and outrage. She explained again that she and Michael had gotten in a quarrel while in bed. Michael redressed, threatening to leave her. That was when she said she talked of killing herself. They wrestled for the gun. It went off somehow. Michael died, but it was just an accident. She fully expected the matter to drop then and there.

It did, for a time. The police advised Elvira that she was free to go. She went home to her parents. But the newspapers were already ordering extra ink to headline the scandal with the likes of "SOCIETY TRAGEDY SENSATION AND KNIGHT'S DAUGHTER ON MURDER CHARGE." Many eyes popped, for the upper crust was not known to run around London shooting people, accidentally or otherwise. Many tongues wagged about the details of the lifestyle of this embarrassing daughter of privilege and rank.

The police then found some witnesses who gave the case a different complexion entirely. One of Elvira's neighbors swore that she heard the shooting, and just before then she heard Mrs. Barney shout, "I'll shoot you!" The same neighbor also remembered an incident that occurred a few days earlier when Mrs. Barney was arguing with Michael. Mrs. Barney was standing at her open bedroom window; Michael was on the ground below. From her position in the window, Elvira shouted, "Laugh, baby. Laugh for the last time." Then she tried to shoot him through the open window.[3] A second neighbor corroborated the story of the first, so three days after the shooting, the London police paid a visit to Belgrave Square and placed Mrs. Barney under arrest for murder to spectacular tabloid effect. London talked of no one else.

It was rumored that her parents sold their Chinese art collection to fund her defense.[4] It must have been quite something, for it purchased the services of the most gifted cross-examiner London's Central Criminal Court has ever seen, one of the best trial lawyers then alive. A mesmerizing speaker and forensic genius who hypnotized London juries and dominated the Old Bailey for decades, Sir Patrick Hastings agreed to try the case for Mrs. Barney. As the judge remarked of Hastings, "If anyone can get her off altogether he is the man to do it."[5]

The trial of *R. v. Barney* began on Monday, July 4, 1932, at the Central Criminal Court in London. The line to enter began to form twenty hours earlier, on Sunday afternoon. Her attorney's first challenge was to get inside the courthouse. "The crowd round the building was something I have never experienced before or since," he later recalled.

In his memoirs, Elvira's attorney also remembered the unusually well-dressed crowd of friends who attended her trial. "The mere evidence of luxury and perhaps refinement which permeated the atmosphere of the Court appeared to accentuate a hundredfold the horror of her position," he said. He actually met Elvira Barney for the first time as the trial began because the defense attorney had the curious habit of refusing to see clients prior to trial. Sir Hastings's first look at his client was disappointing. She made a sad, depressing figure in the dock. "Her appearance was not calculated to move the hearts of a jury," he observed.

Elvira did adopt an appropriate courtroom demeanor. Every time her lover's death was mentioned, Elvira wept. When not weeping, she twisted her handkerchief.

The judge, Justice Travers Humphreys, reigned in his courtroom and probably foresaw the outcome. The judge had the misfortune (if that is the word) of encountering three famous femmes fatales over his long and distinguished legal career. In his thirties, he was associated with the defense of femme fatale Kitty Byron. In his fifties, he prosecuted Mrs. Thompson. Now in his mid-sixties, he was presiding over the trial of Elvira Barney.[6] Elvira was to be tried in the same courtroom where another femme fatale, Madame Fahmy, was tried nine years earlier. Coincidentally, both cases concerned a woman who shot her lover with a revolver and was charged with murder, and in each case, the prosecutor was Percival Clarke. His father, the legendary trial lawyer Sir Edward Clarke, had defended femme fatale Adelaide Bartlett. The prosecutor must have sensed that he had an uphill fight.

The Crown began with its strongest evidence. The neighbors told the jury about the incident where Elvira threatened to shoot her boyfriend before the fatal night. The neighbors overheard the murder and the threats that preceded it. There were aspects of the case suggesting Elvira was jealous of Michael's interest in another woman, which would make hers a *crime passionel*. Then her attorney, Sir Patrick Hastings, took the spotlight. He was at the height of his remarkable cross-examining skills, and the brilliant examiner tore apart the eyewitness testimony. Each of the hapless neighbors eventually agreed that Elvira might have shouted, "I'll shoot!" rather than, "I'll shoot you!" Elvira's very life depended on one word. "I'll shoot!" could be a suicide threat.

The next critical witness was Sir Bernard Spilsbury, the eminent pathologist. Under the prosecutor's direct questioning, Spilsbury testified that Michael Stephen did not shoot himself. Yet neither the prosecutor nor the expert spoke to Elvira's actual defense. Elvira never said Michael shot himself. She had always maintained that they were struggling for the gun when it discharged "by accident."

That is when the brilliant defense attorney earned his fee. When Sir Patrick Hastings stood to cross-examine the expert, he had the attention of a larger audience than those who appeared at the courthouse. He chose a strategy requiring fearless self-confidence in the face of grave danger. The result would be either ridicule or victory. The king of cross-examination chose not to cross-examine Sir Bernard Spilsbury. Onlookers may have been confused, but it was a brilliant strategy. Because the expert never spoke on direct examination about Elvira's version of the story, the Crown had no expert testimony to rebut Elvira's account. The expert knew it too. He stepped down in defeat. Said Sir Hastings, "I never remember to have felt greater pleasure at seeing a witness leave the box."

There was one more expert between Elvira and freedom in the form of a famous firearms examiner. Robert Churchill was called to testify that Elvira's revolver took a lot of pressure to fire and was unlikely to discharge accidentally. On cross, Sir Hastings destroyed this expert by asking questions that were so carefully worded they serve as textbook models of the perfect questioning of an expert. Four deceptively simple questions composed by Sir Hastings were intended to save the life of Elvira Barney:

"Supposing a person had got the revolver and another person came and there was a struggle, it is extremely likely that if they continued to struggle and the revolver was loaded it would go off?"

"Yes," Churchill said.

"And it is quite impossible for anyone who was not there to know exactly how the revolver in these circumstances would go off?"

"Yes."

"And if one person has the revolver in his hand and the other person seizes it and the revolver is pointing towards him, it is certain it will go off if it is pressed hard enough?"

"Yes."

"And if he happened to be there, opposite the resolver, he would be certain to be killed?"

"Yes. Yes, he would; of course."

A second expert left the box in defeat, and Sir Patrick Hastings forever cemented his reputation as one of the most brilliant attorneys to ever appear at the Old Bailey.

The final hurdle in Elvira's struggle to regain her freedom was her own testimony. When it came time for her to take the oath and face the crowded courtroom, Elvira nearly snapped. Her attorney slowly coaxed her into testifying. Together they wove a tale of a woeful marriage and her legal difficulties. She had sought a divorce from her husband, but his status as an American was a complication that left her officially married. Much was made of this unflattering tale because it was the only circumstance of her privileged life that might garner some sympathy with the jury. During the telling, Elvira was "restrained" and kept herself under control. When it came time to testify about her relationship with Michael Stephen, she said she'd been unhappy and had threatened suicide. Her boyfriend threatened to leave her, there was a struggle for the gun, a shot—and he slumped to the floor. As to the specifics, she claimed amnesia. The incident witnessed by neighbors was another suicide attempt on her part. As her attorney would later say, "To my intense relief she told her story extremely well."

Sir Hastings's closing argument for Elvira Barney will always be known as one of the best of its kind. Elvira's attorney mesmerized the jury, his words cutting off the legs of the prosecution's case, dealing blow after blow to the murder theory asserted by the Crown. He had a knack for rebuttal, a way of making sense that all could understand. Nobody saw what actually happened. She had her story of an accident; no one could say otherwise. Immediately after the defense's closing argument, the judge turned to the jury and said, "You have just listened to a great forensic effort. I am not paying compliments when I say it is one of the finest speeches that I have ever heard delivered at the Bar."

That speech saved pretty Elvira Barney's neck. She was acquitted. Flowers were pressed into her hands, and photographers followed the smiling young woman as she departed in triumph.

After her acquittal, her defense attorney saw her once more. A few days after the verdict, he was traveling in his car up a steep road when a long, low car dashed around the corner on the wrong side, "nearly killing me and my chauffeur who was sitting beside me. As he indignantly picked up his cap he said: 'Did you see who was driving that car, sir? It was Mrs. Barney!'"[7]

Regardless of the verdict, Elvira Barney was never freed from the prison of drugs and booze of her own making. She probably would have lived longer had she gone to prison. Instead she died of an alcohol overdose in Paris a mere five years after her trial. Elvira's body was found on her bed, still wearing her fur coat.

✝ ✝ ✝

For more information: Elvira inspired a character by the same name in Noel Coward's 1941 play *Blithe Spirit*. Online, she lives on at Maurice Bottomley's blog, Cocktails with Elvira, elvirabarney.wordpress.com.

ADELAIDE
BARTLETT

THE VICTIM: Thomas Edwin Bartlett
WHEN: January 1, 1886
WHERE: The Pimlico district of London, England
DEFENSE COUNSEL: Sir Edward Clarke

THE CASE

Regina v. Bartlett is one of history's oddest and most unforgettable murder trials. It is the story of a love triangle gone terribly wrong, as love triangles are wont to do. Adelaide, Thomas, and George were not so much star-crossed as double-crossed, and each of them behaved in utterly mystifying ways. From the beginning, there was furious public interest due to the accused killer's "strange relations" with her husband and "yet more strange relations" with their minister. The shocking details have been studied ever since by students of the ménage à trois the world over.

The curious facts concerning the Bartlett marriage could fill a book themselves. Mrs. Bartlett was widely considered a lovely woman, "a pretty, pixyish lady" who had married a man ten years her senior after meeting him exactly once. Moreover, Thomas Bartlett was an odd duck. A hardworking grocer who co-owned a small chain of stores, Mr. Bartlett could not have been more middle class or more Victorian. Yet by many accounts, the self-educated grocer had formed some strange opinions about marriage—strange in his day and age as well as ours. He liked to say, for example, in all seriousness that a man should have two wives, one to take out and one to do the work.

A widely circulated studio portrait of Adelaide Bartlett. Original Artwork: Photo by Russell & Sons. (Hulton Archive/Getty Images.)

Mr. Bartlett married (only once), yet there was trouble from day one between Thomas and Adelaide. According to her, the terms of the marriage did not include intimacy. (This was probably untrue, since she had gotten pregnant—the baby was stillborn—and her husband had four or five condoms in the pockets of his trousers when he died. But she had to have some justification for her questioned conduct.) Suffice it to say there was some hushed-up unpleasantness, rumors that Adelaide had run away more than once, rumors that she had fallen in love with her husband's brother Fred, who had to move to America, and the curious fact that the Bartletts slept in separate rooms. It also came out that the Bartletts owned a book about birth control, *Esoteric Anthropology.* (Because the book was mentioned in connection with the case, 125,000 copies were sold in three months.[1])

Adelaide once confided to a friend (who told the world under oath) some further curious facts about her marriage. Her husband surrounded Adelaide with male acquaintances. He encouraged them to romance his wife. "The more attention and admiration I gained from these male acquaintances," Adelaide confided, "the more delighted did he appear. Their attention to me gave him pleasure, or seemed to give him pleasure."

One day the odd couple went to church. There they met their new Wesleyan minister, Rev. George Dyson. Young and handsome, he was soon a regular at the Bartlett home. Adelaide then began to cuckold her husband—with his full consent. Together they chose the man Adelaide would marry after her husband's death. Thomas Bartlett heartily encouraged the romance between his wife and his minister. Mr. Bartlett even wrote a will leaving his wife everything and making her next husband, Reverend Dyson, the executor of his estate.

One must stop and wonder why Thomas Bartlett did not foresee a risk to his happiness, if not to his life, in this curious love triangle of his own construction. It calls to mind the theories of true crime author F. Tennyson Jesse, who famously coined the word *murderee* to mean one who, being in danger, is utterly unable to save himself, like a bird hypnotized by a snake.[2] Or a man hypnotized by a femme fatale.

A prosecutor would later theorize that Adelaide was anxious to begin her new life as Mrs. Reverend Dyson. If true, she rejoiced when her husband Thomas fell seriously ill for the first time at age forty. When his weeks-long illness did not produce the desired result, Adelaide helped her odd but loving and supportive husband into the next world around the stroke of midnight on New Year's Eve by somehow managing to get him to swallow a massive dose of chloroform. That noxious chemical had been procured for her by her intended, Reverend Dyson.

The new widow failed to divulge her use of the chloroform, which was a mistake on her part. They found at autopsy that his stomach was full of it. Chloroform was declared the cause of Thomas Bartlett's death. Either he took it intentionally to kill himself (ridiculously unlikely; it is a highly caustic chemical) or was first lulled into a stupor with chloroform, then it was poured down his throat. Adelaide would soon admit that she habitually used chloroform on a handkerchief to give her husband some sleep. Suspicion swirled around her.[3]

An inquest was held. Her best friend Mrs. Matthews betrayed a few embarrassing confidences. She testified that Adelaide complained about Mr. Bartlett's sexual demands and said she used chloroform on her husband to cool his ardor. Then Reverend Dyson turned on her. He gave inquest testimony that incriminated Mrs. Bartlett. As soon as the minister's testimony ended, she was arrested. Reverend Dyson had testified that he asked Adelaide after her husband's death if she used chloroform

A wood engraving ca. 1886 depicts Adelaide Bartlett. (From the Wellcome Library, London.) In *Defender's Triumph*, true crime author Edgar Lustgarten described Adelaide Bartlett as "too beautiful to be pretty, too pretty to be beautiful. . . . A charming girl, to become a fascinating woman, baited with allurement for the hungry, youthful male."

on him, and she said she did not use it. Then she asked him to forget all about buying any chloroform for her. When he learned that chloroform was the cause of death, he confronted Adelaide. She responded angrily, and they never saw each other outside a courtroom again.[4]

When she went on trial in the Old Bailey, Adelaide Bartlett was represented by that master of cross-examination, Sir Edward Clarke, the best trial lawyer since Cicero.[5] Few lawyers have such luminescence that they can light up a dry, dusty trial transcript, but Sir Clarke was one of the rare few.[6] The case was challenging for the defense, no matter how pretty Adelaide Bartlett was. The *who*, *what*, *when*, *where*, and *why* of this murder mystery were perfectly clear, but not so the *how* of it. The defense attorney aimed carefully at the only weakness in the Crown's case against Adelaide. He was so extraordinarily well prepared and masterful in his cross of the medical men that by the end of the trial, the jury perceived that killing someone with chloroform was very difficult to pull off. Sir Clarke quoted numerous medical journals that supported the defense's point: Even the best medical minds had not mastered the vagaries of volatile, caustic liquid chloroform.[7] His cross-examination of the Crown's medical experts set an international standard for the interrogation of medical witnesses.[8]

To believe the defense theory, the jury had to ignore the testimony of those who said Adelaide had the advantage of practice, for she had been administering chloroform to poor Tom Bartlett "to cool his ardor" for some time. Had she gained enough experience administering chloroform to her husband to have some mastery over the stuff?

Her attorney had the last word. In his brilliant closing argument, Sir Clarke declared, "Gentlemen, whatever the history of our medical jurisprudence may be, this case will long be remembered." Since chloroform's anesthetic properties were discovered forty years before, it had never been used as a weapon. "This is the first case that the world has ever heard of in which it has been suggested that a person has been murdered by the administration of liquid chloroform. Adelaide Bartlett has committed an offence absolutely unknown in the history of medical jurisprudence. You are asked to believe that that woman, that night, alone with her husband, performed on him this marvelous operation."[9]

The jurors did not believe it. They did not deliberate long before they acquitted Adelaide. The poisoner had been caught and proven to be a liar, but she had also been spared. Adelaide fainted as the courtroom erupted in approval.[10]

Decades after the controversial defense verdict, some still wonder what became of her. Most researchers come to a dead end with her trial. Some say she ended up in America. Some believe she went to South Africa with Lady Churchill's nurses. Some point to the seventeen marriage proposals she received immediately after the jury declared itself blind to her faults.

Sir James Paget, an eminent medical expert, would have the last word. He famously declared after the trial, "Now that it's all over, she should tell us, in the interests of science, how she did it."

COUNTESS
LINDA MURRI
BONMARTINI

THE VICTIM: Count Francesco Bonmartini
WHEN: August 28, 1902
WHERE: Bologna, Italy
DEFENSE COUNSEL: Giuseppe Gottardi

THE CASE

Here is a complicated tale of a femme fatale who came to be known in her native Italy as "the Enchantress." She was wealthy and well bred, and if not very beautiful, then at least pleasing to the eye, and she committed some of the most forbidden acts imaginable. Four men were passionately in love with Linda—her husband, her lover, her brother, and her father. "According to credible sources," states Murri expert Christina Vella, "her husband was the only one with whom she was not having sexual relations."[1] When one of the four wound up dead, this remarkable woman came to the attention of an amazed world, causing "great excitement" across the globe.[2]

The legal mystery began with a powerful odor emanating from the home of the husband of the Enchantress. Count Francesco Bonmartini was found very dead in the foyer of his Bologna residence. He was covered in stab wounds inflicted by various instruments. He had been attacked by a mob, it seemed, and suffered an agonizing, tortured, horrible death. The first of fifteen blows had pierced his heart.[3]

If he was not a notorious libertine before he died, he is forever remembered as one. Police found his correspondence and learned he had not one or two but three girlfriends (Nini, Silvia, and Clelia), still patronized low women, and was preoccupied with his perversions. Then they learned that the count had predicted his murder to friends. Two days before he was killed, he bought himself a coffin and a grave.

Countess Linda Murri Bonmartini made headlines across the world and is featured here in the *Auckland (New Zealand) Star,* August 16, 1909. (Public domain, via Newspaperarchive.com.)

The riddle was unsolved until the father of Countess Bonmartini went to the police and denounced his own son, attorney Tullio Murri, as the killer. Tullio soon confessed and accepted all the blame. Yet the police were reading trunks full of correspondence, uncovering a vast conspiracy. It clearly appeared that the victim was detested by his wife and her family circle, and they decided as an ensemble that Count Bonmartini had to die.[4]

The countess was taken into custody. The countess's lover, Dr. Carlo Secchi, was arrested. Apparently, the countess had accepted the aid of a lover (actually, two lovers, counting her brother) in the murder of her husband. Then Tullio's inamorata, Rosina Bonetti, was arrested. Tullio's friend, Dr. Pio Naldi, was arrested. The case caused such an uproar in their native Bologna that it had to be transferred to the court in Turin.

What followed was one of the most shocking murder trials in Italian history. The criminal proceedings were an epistolary study, since most of the evidence of the intrigues among the many defendants consisted of the correspondence between them. The countess's father and brother were quite obsessed with her. Both men wrote amazing love letters to her. The florid declarations of adoration confirmed the rumors of a deeper degeneracy between them. There was no reasonable doubt that they could have been convicted on an incest charge. These letters caused some to call the countess a "sickness that infected others."[5] Yet much was said of the debauchery of the dead man, and the countess through her attorney told a pitiful tale of a miserable marriage to an inhuman monster who committed acts that were worse than incestuous.

After six months of trial with four hundred witnesses, at last the jury made its decision. Each of the five defendants was found guilty and sentenced from ten to thirty years. The jury concluded that Tullio Murri was the person who actually stabbed his brother-in-law to death. His friend Pio Naldi helped him. They drew the longest sentences. Countess Linda Murri Bonmartini claimed she did not think it would go so far, but it was still her fault that they did it, the jury concluded. Both the countess and her lover Secchi were convicted for their part in the drama. The countess was convicted of facilitating the murder, and she received a sentence of ten years for her role in killing her husband. The maid Rosina Bonetti loved Tullio and did as he bid her for a term of seven years, her moral failures also contributing to the tragedy. It was said that a majority of the public favored the verdict and prison terms.

But that sentence was all for show, at least for the countess. She was out of prison in a few years, or as soon as her influential father could arrange her release on account of "poor health." Her health wasn't so poor that she couldn't take up with a man again. It was soon announced that she was to marry another.

The lasting mystery is how Countess Linda Murri Bonmartini managed to enthrall every man who ever knew her.

✝ ✝ ✝

For more information: Catherine Deneuve played Countess Bonmartini in the 1974 film *The Murri Affair* (*La grand bourgeoise*).

KITTY BYRON

A highly popular murder had been committed. . . .
—Charles Dickens, *Great Expectations*

THE VICTIM: Arthur Reginald Baker
WHEN: November 10, 1902
WHERE: London, England
DEFENSE COUNSEL: Henry Fielding Dickens and Sir Travers
Humphreys

THE CASE

After a fight with her lover, Emma Byron went shopping for a sharp knife and then stabbed him in the heart with it. When she was "hauled to the bench" at the Old Bailey to answer for her hideous crime, she struck onlookers who knew her whole story as pitiable . . . and yet attractive.

It was "the most pathetic case in which I have ever been concerned," declared her defense counsel, Sir Travers Humphreys. The truth was, the victim had treated Emma "Kitty" Byron quite badly. Kitty was living in hopeless conditions with her boyfriend Arthur Baker, a married stockbroker, in London. He was a drunken lout, according to neutral witnesses, and had already abandoned his wife. When drunk, he liked to beat his girlfriend Kitty. Now he intended to discard her. The testimony of their landlady would set the scene. "When he was sober, he was a perfect gentleman," their landlady told a hushed courtroom, "but he was very seldom sober." Every night he beat Kitty. "I have heard him say many times that he would kill her."

Arthur Baker was served with divorce papers on November 7, 1902. Naturally this raised questions about his intentions and future plans.

This led to days of fighting.[1] After a severe argument, the landlady told them to leave for good. Arthur declared that it was Kitty, who was "no class," who would be leaving—moving back in with her mother. Yet Kitty wouldn't go. "I cannot leave him," she told the landlady, "because I love him."[2] With this tale of woe Kitty struck the hearts of listeners.

Kitty Byron was greatly pitied. Arthur Baker was greatly loathed. She was young and pretty, and this wealthy, married stockbroker had mercilessly ruined her.

Numerous witnesses would firmly establish that some short time after their last argument, on November 10, 1902, Kitty went shopping in Oxford Street for a sharp knife. Then she sent word for Arthur Baker to meet her outside the Lombard Street post office, where they argued. The knife materialized, and she plunged the sharp new blade into Arthur's chest. He fell to the ground, killed by the hand of Kitty Byron.

An accountant passing by saw the attack. "I smiled," he later said, "as I thought it was a domestic matter," because violence by women against men is turnabout, which is not only fair play but amusing, apparently, "but on seeing him fall, and that she had a weapon, I became aware that it was serious."

At the conclusion of the evidence, one fact was clear—Kitty Byron had committed a premeditated murder. Then the lawyers gave their summations.

Kitty Byron had the best defense attorneys money could buy. Not on an assistant milliner's pay, of course; her defense was funded by none other than the members of the London Stock Exchange, where the murder victim had worked.[3] In other words, the murder victim's fellow stockbrokers took on the responsibility of treating Kitty Byron well when their brother broker had failed. Any number of motives may explain the Stock Exchange's decision, but its public support for Kitty Byron was intended to save her neck. The Exchange retained two attorneys on her behalf. One was young but already taking on legendary proportions, Sir Travers Humphreys. Her other learned counsel was Henry Fielding Dickens, son of literary phenomenon and true crime maven Charles Dickens. It was said that the junior Dickens "had inherited all his father's dramatic force, together with a charming manner and a delightful personality which endeared him to all who knew or heard him."[4]

For his closing speech in the trial of Miss Byron, Dickens retold her tragic tale, the story of a knife that plunged into a man's chest as if guided by an occult hand. His speech was "a masterpiece. Beautifully delivered, it was frankly less of an argument than an appeal to both the judge and the jury," said his brother counsel Sir Humphreys. When Dickens spoke for the defense, the Old Bailey could not have admitted one more person.

Dickens wove a tale of a woman who bought a knife to kill herself, or at least to threaten her own life with it. He suggested she was just the sort of hysterical neurotic woman who might have killed herself. "See how she loved the man," Dickens declared. "It is only another case of where the love of woman passes understanding. With him when beaten, when half strangled, when rich or poor, for good or evil, she loved him because she knew that, when he was sober, he loved her."

The judge was having none of it. He swept aside the Dickensian view of the case and the whole idea that Kitty Byron was somehow not responsible for the public stabbing of Arthur Baker. The judge gave instructions to the jury directing that on these facts, Miss Byron was guilty of murder. The judge may have known a few things about Kitty Byron that the prosecution had chosen not to attempt to use against her. It was said that there was evidence of her "bisexual past and unstable mentality."[5] The jury duly found her guilty—but recommended mercy.

Her judge put on the black cap. The pronouncement was a foregone conclusion. She may have been twenty-four years old, and she may have been very pretty, but in Edwardian England, facts were facts, the evidence could be subject to just one interpretation, and there was no reasonable doubt. The judge pronounced her sentence: Death.

That of course was for show. Even the prosecutor knew as the sentence was being pronounced that she was too pretty to execute.[6] She served six years and was out by age thirty. Rumor had it that it was later proved "she had quite a violent character."[7]

Sadly, Kitty Byron was never to be photographed for the public. A single sketch has been enough for her pretty face to transfix the true crime set for ages.

FLORENCE CARMAN

THE VICTIM: Louise "Lulu" Bailey
WHEN: June 30, 1914
WHERE: Freeport, Long Island, New York
DEFENSE COUNSEL: George M. Levy

THE CASE

In 1914, a panel of grand jurors convened to investigate the mysterious shooting death of Louise "Lulu" Bailey. One night that summer, Mrs. Bailey arranged an after-hours visit with her physician, Dr. Edwin Carman, at his office on the ground floor of his luxurious Long Island mansion. During that visit, someone fired a shot through the window. The bullet killed Lulu Bailey.

The horrified doctor saw nothing. The only eyewitness to the murder was a passing tramp. Frank Farrell offered the observation that a woman in a flowing robe had committed the crime. This led to predictable speculation regarding Mr. Farrell's mental state.

Then came the testimony of Miss Celia Coleman. It was one thing to talk to the police. It was quite another, apparently, to swear on a Holy Bible to tell the truth to a panel of grand jurors. What Celia Coleman said, for the first time, shocked everyone who heard it. Before this day came, she told police she knew nothing. But she knew everything.

This is what Celia Coleman swore. She was working as a live-in maid for the Carmans. She testified that Mrs. Carman, the doctor's wife, had been extremely kind to her. Florence Carman was a beauty, always

This portrait of Florence Carman was taken between 1910 and 1915. (From the George Grantham Bain Collection [Library of Congress].)

impeccably dressed for the occasion. One night, while the maid was working in the kitchen of the Carman household, she was surprised by the sudden appearance of the doctor's wife. "Mrs. Carman came into the kitchen dressed in a kimono," she testified. "She went out the back door. I heard a crash of glass and report of a pistol. Mrs. Carman came in the same door. She said: 'I shot him.' She showed me a revolver."

To a hushed room, this disinterested and compelling witness, a maid, a dignified, well-dressed, decent-looking woman with no motive to destroy another life, continued: "The next morning she came to my room. She said: 'Oh, Celia, what did I kill that woman for? I hope God will forgive me.' She told me to forget what I saw.

These photographs of eyewitness Celia Coleman were probably taken out-side the courthouse in Mineola, Long Island, New York. (From the George Grantham Bain Collection [Library of Congress].)

"The next day she told me to call her father from the barn. She said she wanted to get the revolver out of the house."

Celia Coleman was subjected to a withering cross-examination. She did not change a syllable of her testimony, even when the lawyer for the doctor's wife left her in tears. She never wavered. She never raised her voice.[1]

Florence Carman was arrested. Police investigated her, desperate to establish some motive for the bizarre crime, when jealousy reared its ugly head. They soon learned that Mrs. Carman had installed a Dicta-phone in her husband's medical office. With it, she could eavesdrop on his office visits. On the night of the crime, she was aflame with jealousy, convinced that he was in his examining room trysting with his mistress.[2]

With that, Florence Carman was arrested and went on trial for her life.

The twelve male jurors who were chosen to hear her case swore that they could listen to Celia Coleman's testimony without thinking of ancient prejudices. The journalists, though, could not help themselves. In most headlines generated by the case, Celia Coleman was noted to be a "Negro."

As any femme fatale worth the title could attest, though, the evidence did not matter. Florence Carman was handsome, poised, and dignified during the trial. Her husband, daughter, family, and friends stood by her, their presence resting heavily on the jurors. Her mother, sister, and daughter all testified that Mrs. Carman was in bed at the time of the shooting. That was enough. An all-male jury would never send such a woman to the electric chair for a crime of passion regardless of the quality of the evidence against her. "So strong and so universal is the masculine aversion to the death penalty for women that in the year 1912 no woman was executed anywhere in the world."[3]

Mrs. Carman was sanguine in her summation of the case: "The law has harried my soul," Florence testified. "It has held me up as an accused murderess to the scorn of all the public, and heaven knows the public has sometimes been cruel in its attitude toward me. But I respect the law and honor the public nevertheless."

The jury set her free, of course. Florence may have shot and killed a woman who was a stranger to her, but she had the advantage of a New York venue for her murder trial. New York was a death penalty state. Rarely were women executed there. The very idea repulsed the public. Juries found it easier to cling to any old excuse rather than bring themselves to call for a woman's execution, even if it did mean setting a killer free and dishonoring the victim. In New York, this was old news. As one journalist had observed generations earlier, "Of late years quite a number of females in New York, who had grievances against men, promptly rectified them by shooting large apertures in the anatomical structures of the offending representatives of the male sex with fatal results. In the last two cases sympathetic juries acquitted the fair shootists with such promptness that it would not have created surprise if the jurymen had chipped in and presented the acquitted woman with a silver-mounted pistol, properly inscribed. It may come to that yet if we keep on as we are going."[4]

It was said that after her acquittal, Dr. Carman fixed the broken window in his office and resumed his practice as though nothing untoward had ever happened there. Mrs. Carman and her husband resumed their upper-class lives, going to the club, the Methodist church, and the homes of loyal friends. Everyone who was anyone in Freeport welcomed her back to society. One is left to wonder how either of them ever slept again.

JESSIE COSTELLO

What do you think women are? Flowers? Take that dame that
shot the dentist! And Mrs. Vermilya! Husband comes home,
all worn out, hungry, takes a spoonful of soup, and falls dead!
Arsenic! And Mrs. Petras! Burning her husband up in a furnace!
When you've been in this business as long as I have, you'll know
what women are! Murderers! Borgias!

—Newspaper editor Walter Burns's lines from *The
Front Page,* by Ben Hecht and Douglas MacArthur

THE VICTIM: William J. Costello
WHEN: February 17, 1933
WHERE: Peabody, Massachusetts
DEFENSE COUNSEL: William G. Clark and Frances E. Rafter

THE CASE

Illicit affairs that end in tragedy, detailed at length and under oath,
make for fascinating courtroom proceedings. Here is a murder trial so
lurid that a British expert once declared it "the most amazing piece
of criminal jurisprudence within the last fifty years."[1] The *New Yorker*
agreed that it was "as luscious a trial as any in the gaudy annals of
American jurisprudence."[2] It has even been called the Perfect American Trial. That might be overstating the case, since the obnoxious verdict does not entirely surprise those who know the *lex non scripta.*

Jessie Costello was a handsome woman married to a Peabody fire
captain. They seemed well suited for each other, and they had four children. This seemingly harmless housewife lived on Fay Avenue with her
family and father-in-law when two tragedies struck her. The couple's

This photo by renowned *Boston Herald-Traveler* photographer Leslie Jones shows the overflow crowds at Jessie Costello's trial. (Courtesy of the Boston Public Library, Leslie Jones Collection. Used with permission of the Estate of Leslie Jones.)

youngest child, a little boy, died. A short time later, her husband was found dead of no obvious cause.

The town of Peabody reviewed everything it knew of the Costellos. Jessie, dressed in black, made for a "comely widow," as the press put it. Townsfolk said Mr. Costello was a serious, home-loving, family-focused man, and Jessie, not so much. As the whole town (and later, the entire world) would soon come to know, one day Jessie had driven by a gift to Peabody's womankind. He was a handsome young police officer. He was on traffic duty, and he was also a good friend of her husband.

She brought her car to a halt and asked, "How would you like to be in here?"

"I wouldn't mind," he responded.

That is how her affair began with a married policeman, Bill McMahon. She called him "Big Boy." Jessie and Bill trysted in her car five nights in a row and then regularly, having sex about every day from November to mid-February.[3] He would one day testify about the details to a shocked courtroom, telling everyone that Jessie "was continually talking sex."[4] Then her husband died of no apparent cause. Suddenly everyone in the Western world was continually talking Jessie Costello.

Rumor said she had run up debts. Rumor had it that her husband had discovered the truth about her affair and had confronted her. He was quoted as shouting, "Haven't you any brains? Can't you let that boy alone?" Another report had it that less than two hours passed from the time Mrs. Costello discovered her husband's body until the time she was reviewing his $5,000 worth of life insurance policies at the fire station, ably demonstrating that as her husband suspected, she hadn't any brains.

The acquittal of Jessie B. Costello in an extra edition with a banner headline. From the *Fitchburg (Massachusetts) Sentinel*, August 15, 1933, via Newspaper archive.com.

Another extra edition announces the Costello verdict. (From the *Lowell [Massachusetts] Sun*, August 15, 1933, via Newspaperarchive.com.)

A triumphant Jessie Costello poses for the press after her acquittal. (Courtesy of the Boston Public Library, Leslie Jones Collection. Used with permission of the Estate of Leslie Jones.)

Then it was discovered that she had recently bought empty capsules. The police investigation took on a new intensity. Her lover Bill McMahon was questioned; he gave up every delicious detail of their affair.

An autopsy was ordered. The postmortem examination found that William Costello had consumed cyanide. His widow declared she bought it the day before his death to clean their boiler. Everyone with a lick of common sense saw all this for what it was—a cold-blooded murder by poison. The Boston area press "went stark, raving mad."[5]

Jessie's trial took place in Salem, Massachusetts, where in a prior time a character like her would have been hanged within a week. She could be thankful that the twentieth century had so far treated pretty husband-poisoners with lenience. England had offered its example in Beatrice Pace, who was accused and acquitted of committing mariticide with arsenic to tremendous public acclaim.[6] For poisoner Jessie

Costello, the crowds may have been the thickest ever to beset the Salem courthouse. Scores of reporters, novelists, artists, lawyers, and miscellaneous others were attracted to the spectacle of an attractive woman accused of the deliberate murder of a loyal husband, loving father, and fireman—and by poison no less. Jessie's figure parted onlookers as she entered and exited the courthouse. She returned the many smiles aimed at her, seemingly oblivious to the danger she was in, for she had violated one of the rules for murderesses by having a lover in evidence.

Then a brilliant attorney came to rescue this damsel in legal distress. William G. Clark agreed to represent her. Her only hope of a defense lay in challenging what was largely indirect evidence. The prosecutor followed that old adage that a circumstantial case can be strong, as when, to use Thoreau's phrase, you find a trout in the milk. Jessie Costello's defense attorney expertly skewered the commonwealth's case for the lack of any direct evidence of Jessie's guilt. Besides her affair, there was no suggestion of a motive for Jessie to murder the father of her children. His insurance policy was not a large one. A circumstantial case is only as strong as its weakest link, her attorney argued, and Jessie was greatly in love with her husband. Any evidence to the contrary was a lie.

"I loved Bill and Bill loved me," she said, referring to her husband and not her lover of the same first name. She denied everything else said of her. "Never in my life have I so much as touched the person."

The highlight of Jessie's four-day trial was the humiliation of her lover. Thousands turned out to claim seating for a few hundred. On the witness stand, Officer McMahon was forced to reveal how Mrs. Costello had pursued him and refused to let him end their affair.

"I protested with her about seeing me so much," he admitted. "I said our affair was getting to be common talk. I told her a friend of mine had advised me that for my own sake I should stop seeing her, especially as Bill was such a good friend of mine. She looked at me and said: 'Don't be silly.'"[7]

"It's all a mess of lies," said the defiant defendant.

The jury applied its collective masculine logic to the case and came to a unanimous decision. Jessie was acquitted entirely. Onlookers expressed their deep shock, but eventually the crowd rose to a standing ovation. After setting her free, the jurors chipped in and sent the acquitted poisoner a box of candy.

The verdict should not have been a surprise to anyone inside or outside the courtroom. As one historian observed, "It was a period when accused husband-murderers—provided they were pretty—were invariably acquitted."[8] Yet some newspaper editors disagreed. Outrage met the verdict since it was obvious that the odds of her innocence were the same as the odds of finding any other housewife in all of New England who cleaned her boiler with cyanide. The editors railed against her after the verdict, suggesting she go home and stay there. Furthermore, she should be ashamed of all the rumors of her upcoming stage debut as an actress with no claim to fame other than being deservedly accused of making orphans of her children and cruelly ending the life of her devoted, faultless husband. "Many people were astonished," noted true crime author Edmund L. Pearson, "but they cynically attributed the verdict to the fact that twelve male jurors sat for weeks in close proximity to the prisoner, and as helpless as twelve rabbits under the influence of those glittering ophidian[9] eyes."

SUSAN CUMMINGS

THE VICTIM: Roberto Cerillio Villegas
WHEN: September 7, 1997
WHERE: Warrenton, Virginia
DEFENSE COUNSEL: Blair D. Howard

THE CASE

To the four men and ten women chosen as jurors and alternates in the trial of Susan Cummings, she must have seemed like a character from a fairy tale. Gentle, well bred, and shy, she was a woman who loved animals, collected cats and horses, and kept her television tuned to Animal Planet. She spoke (when she did speak) with a Continental accent. Moreover, she was wealthy beyond the imagination of ordinary people.

Susan (she preferred it pronounced *Su-ZAHN*) was born in France as the daughter of an international arms dealer who was one of the richest men in the world. Susan and her twin sister were raised on the French Riviera, where she learned to shoot a gun when she was five years old. The twins attended college together at a posh all-girls' school near Washington, DC, Mount Vernon College, and then settled together in Virginia's exclusive horse country on a magnificent 350-acre horse farm purchased for them by their father. Susan could have anything in life she could possibly want. When she needed a tractor for her farm, she ordered an $80,000 model and paid for it with her credit card.

All of this only made it a grave surprise when on a lovely autumn morning Susan Cummings, thirty-five, phoned 911 and uttered a spectacularly passive sentence in her prettily accented English: "I need to report a . . . a shot man and he's dead." When asked if she had shot him, she said, "I had a gun, yes." According to the forensic experts, she shot her boyfriend four times while he was seated at her kitchen table, chewing his last bite of breakfast.

Born in a village near Córdoba, Argentina, Roberto Villegas was the son of a poor farmhand who was raised by a loving family in a home with no utilities. He grew up playing polo, a popular sport in that nation and one in which he excelled. At twenty-one, he left Argentina with a seventh-grade education and immigrated to the United States to play polo for the wealthy. Known for being handsome, flirtatious, and an aggressive player who was occasionally thrown out of polo matches, in time he came to find himself playing on the team of one of the richest heiresses in the world, Susan Cummings.

The opposites were attracted to one another. For a time, they seemed very happy, and Roberto even felt a little sorry for his poor little rich girlfriend. He was known to make remarks about her such as, "She had a hard childhood. Her family was cold, and she was sent away to school when she was only 12 years old." Yet they remained quite unalike. Truth be told, Susan was considered a strange woman. Despite her wealth, she was embarrassingly frugal, occasionally awkward, and often aloof. Acquaintances described her as reserved, quiet, and "so weird." Her voice was often inaudible, and she had a tendency to look at her shoes when she spoke. Her one abiding passion was animals. She kept stuffed animals on her bed—and a .357 Magnum beneath the mattress, along with two more guns in her messy bedroom and another in the kitchen.

Soon enough, the cracks began to appear in the foundation of the relationship between Susan and her handsome polo player. The quirks particular to Susan's personality became burrs under the saddle of the handsome Argentine. As he told a friend, "One day we will get married, but it is many years down the road. All she wants to do is mother me." Little disagreements grew into arguments. Tensions became grudges. Roberto was never allowed to spend the night at his girlfriend's house, even after two years of dating.

As the relationship crumbled, Susan tried to have Roberto deported. Failing that, she visited the local sheriff to complain that she was frightened of him. She had tried to break things off, she said, and Roberto was threatening to kill her. Given his criminal record, she worried that he might make good on the threat. The sheriff who heard her tale ran Roberto's name through a criminal database and found no such criminal record. For this and other reasons, he thought the whole story was hinky. Even so, he offered to assist her in obtaining a restraining order. She politely declined, puzzling the police again. As wealthy as she was, she could have simply had the man forcibly removed from her life. She could have hired bodyguards. She could have done any number of things to protect herself. She did not do those things.

Two weeks later, on his last day of life, Roberto left his rented room in the early morning as he usually did for the short drive to Susan's estate. As he ate breakfast at her kitchen table, a disagreement may have ensued. It was also possible that Roberto was merely reading a magazine that lay open on the table before him. One thing certainly happened that Sunday morning: Susan grabbed her 9mm semiautomatic Walther P1 pistol and ended their relationship.

When Susan reported Roberto's death to authorities, she claimed they got in a terrible argument and Roberto attacked her with a knife. The police photographed what she represented as defense wounds, which were bleeding but did not require medical attention. They did not look like defense wounds to the police. Susan had about a dozen parallel slashes down the length of her left arm. To the practiced eye, the wounds looked superficial and self-inflicted. Defense wounds are not parallel and of the same length. Defense wounds ought to show some evidence of flinching from the edge of the blade.

It appeared to police that Roberto had been shot while seated, and he had then slumped to the floor where they found him, partially under the breakfast table and facedown in a pool of blood. He had gunshot wounds in his neck and chest. There were no signs of a struggle. Investigators would later discern that the paths of the bullets through his body were all downward, affirming their theory that he was sitting in a chair when he was killed.

Susan Cummings was arrested and charged with murder to the delight of the tabloids. Journalists from the *Washington Post, New York Times,* and from as far away as Argentina were following the proceedings. As one scholar of the case has remarked, "The opulent setting, the vast fortune of the Cummings family, and the intrigue of a romance between a wealthy patron and her dashing Argentine polo pro were a magic combination to editors at the nation's top newspapers and television stations."[1]

The preferential treatment for the pretty heiress began immediately: She was released on $75,000 bail. The limit on her credit card was higher than that. Roberto's friends were outraged, certain that if it had been Roberto who had shot Susan, there would be no bail at all. Her few friends defended her and claimed her boyfriend had a temper and Susan wanted to end the relationship. His many friends called this nonsense and said *he* wanted to end the relationship.

To the prosecutor, it seemed an open-and-shut case. But Susan Cummings was a very beautiful woman, and his trial strategy did not account for the *lex non scripta*. Susan also retained the best attorney in the region and one of the best in the country, a man who knew how to defend a would-be femme fatale. With all of her father's money at her disposal, she retained attorney Blair Howard. He is one of the most famous criminal defense attorneys in the Commonwealth of Virginia and indeed the United States, known for taking on seemingly hopeless cases and winning them.[2]

Howard's opening statement to the jury set the tone for what was to come. "This case is not about cold photographs and scientific theory," he said. "This case is about human emotion. The hand that held the dagger struck, and Susan Cummings acted within the law, in her own home, to protect herself in self-defense."

Susan testified through her heavy French accent. She explained to the jury that Roberto was violent and unpredictable. She claimed he once kicked her in the crotch during an argument. He said if she didn't agree to marry him and have his children, he would kill her. She testified that her boyfriend's death came about because she tried to get him to leave. He was going to a polo match that morning, and Susan decided he would have to go without the benefit of taking her horses as he usually did.

"I told Roberto in my calm way," Susan testified. "I said, 'Roberto, I know you have a [polo] game. And if you may, you can go to the game, but you cannot take. . . . you have to make different arrangements for the horses because I am. . . . you cannot take the horses to the game."

"What, if anything, was his reaction to that, ma'am?" her lawyer asked her.

"Roberto became very angry. . . . In a split second, he retrieved the knife, and in a. . . . in a quick minute later, he reached across the table, he took hold of my neck and put the knife at my face. . . . I did not react. I was very fearful, and I. . . . I stayed completely motionless. He pressed the knife against my cheek. . . . He insulted me. . . . He began to scratch my arm, slowly laughing about the fear on my face.

"I didn't want to say 'scratch,'" she corrected herself. "I wanted to say 'slash.'

"My heart was beating," she continued. "I felt my blood rushing down. I felt extremely scared. I felt that my life was in danger. I felt. . . . I thought to myself, this is . . . this man is going to kill me."

On cross-examination, she admitted her act. She could not pretend that the gun was fired without her firing it, as if guided by an occult hand. "I shot him," she said. "I started shooting and I don't know at what point I stopped." She continued: "I never intended for Roberto to get shot. I needed to get this man out of my life."

In the end, the jury found her guilty of voluntary manslaughter. In the Commonwealth of Virginia the jury fixes the punishment, and the panel decided to sentence Susan Cummings to sixty days in jail for killing her boyfriend. With time off for good behavior, she was released after fifty-one days behind bars.

"I feel very happy," she said when the result was announced.

GERMAINE
D'ANGLEMONT

THE VICTIM: Jean Causeret
WHERE: Paris, France
WHEN: March 7, 1933

THE CASE

She was born to a working-class single mother and entered prostitution as "Nini" on the rue des Archives. An encounter with famous author Pierre Decourcelle led her to change her name and move to the Champs-Élysées.[1] From there she practiced her wiles on a succession of ever more successful men until she was the muse of artists, the darling of generals, the sweetheart of men of rank and privilege. Along the way she took a *mari complaisant*[2] and became friends with Mata Hari.[3] By the time she reached full maturity, her lively personality and sexual allure made Germaine d'Anglemont known as one of the most captivating of the Parisian *demimondaines*.[4] Over the years she marked among her triumphs in seduction Prince Franz Josef of Bavaria, a president of Mexico, and a Polish count.[5]

By the time she was forty-five, Germaine more or less settled down to one husband and one lover. She enjoyed *le cinq à sept*[6] with Jean Causeret, a married man who was the prefect of the Rhône. Their love affair was a tortured one, at least at the end. Germaine, of all people, the noted Germaine d'Anglemont who had enjoyed *un rendezvous galant*[7] with man after man, became suspicious of her lover. It was said that Jean was straying, so Germaine hired a woman to follow him. She learned he was not at work as he was supposed to be but was buying gifts at a department store. That night, when they were alone in her apartment, she shot her lover dead.

But she was French. There is an old tradition in French jurisprudence to *cherchez la femme,* and then when you have caught her, to declare her against all logic and evidence *"non coupable!"* In addition, Germaine was beautiful. She followed the rules for murderesses. There was no evidence of premeditation or any ulterior motive other than wild-eyed jealousy. *Vanity Fair* called the brutal death of Jean Causeret a "stylish assassination."[8]

Afterward she claimed it was an accident, but the evidence of her jealous motive could not be ignored entirely.[9] Had a man conducted himself as she had done, there would be no question. Germaine went on trial at the Assize Court in Paris in April 1935. She did what every well-advised French femme fatale would do in that dock, which is to tell a pitiful life story and shed copious tears.[10] Bouquets of flowers appeared from admirers who could not wait for the legendary beauty to leave the dock.

Leave it she did, and as a free woman, free to take up again with wealthy lovers and peddle her romantic correspondence and memoirs. One is tempted to cry, *Vive la différence!* Except that one cannot quite pinpoint *la différence* in the French reaction to the wiles of a femme fatale.

BLANCA
DE SAULLES

THE VICTIM: John Longer de Saulles
WHEN: August 3, 1917
WHERE: Long Island, New York
DEFENSE COUNSEL: Henry A. Uterhart

THE CASE

Blanca and Jack got in their umpteenth argument over the day-to-day custody of their son. This last time, Blanca brought a .32. Confronting her ex-husband in front of a room full of witnesses, she declared, "If I can't have my boy, take this." She emptied the gun into him. Then she calmly took a seat in the garden and waited for the police to arrive.

Jack de Saulles was rushed to the hospital, but he could not overcome his wounds. His last words were, "My wife shot me. I want you to have her arrested. She shot me."

In custody, Blanca asked, "Will they electrocute me right away?"

But it was not to be. "Million-dollar defendants," said one scholar of the case, "get million-dollar defenses."[1]

Years before that fatal moment, Jack de Saulles was Yale's All-American starting quarterback. Upon graduation, he went into real estate, but his true passions lay elsewhere; he had a reputation as a notorious rake. Blanquita Errázuriz-Vergara was half his age, the daughter of a prominent family in Chile, an "Andean princess" rumored to be one of the richest women in South America and one of the loveliest ladies in the world. She was pale and small, a little ivory figurine of a woman. When their paths crossed, Jack wooed and won her, asking her widowed mother for her hand in marriage with a promise that they would not move to the United States. They married in Paris on December 13, 1911, and the wedding made international news. Jack soon fell out with his mother-in-law

Blanca de Saulles posing for the press. (From the George Grantham Bain Collection [Library of Congress].)

over access to the family fortune and promptly moved his bride to New York. On Christmas Day, 1913, she gave birth to Jack Jr. But the marriage was already coming undone. She claimed he neglected and humiliated her with his flagrantly debauched lifestyle.

That's not to say Blanca didn't attend parties and have fun. According to rumors, she had a passionate affair with the sexiest man then alive, Rudolph Valentino, when he was still Rodolfo Guglielmi, fresh off the boat and working in New York as a tango dancer. It was all but public that the soon-to-be Hollywood icon fell madly in love with Blanca while both were in New York.[2] In fact, Valentino testified as a witness in Blanca's headline-making divorce case against Jack. Valentino's testimony—that Jack de Saulles had an affair with his dance partner—helped Blanca establish grounds for divorce and obtain custody of her son. It was proven that Jack was habitually adulterous, yet Blanca was ordered by the final divorce decree to stay in the United States and share custody of their boy with Jack. She was bitter and felt trapped.

Then she attended the murder trial of Florence Carman in June 1914. Mrs. Carman was accused of shooting at her husband, missing, and killing his female companion instead. While watching the Carman trial, Blanca learned about an unwritten law in her adopted country. "In early twentieth-century America," as one observer stated, "trying to gain a murder conviction against any female defendant was tough enough; trying to put a white, middle-class woman in the electric chair was frankly impossible." This meant that any respectable woman had "the emotional license to kill any errant male with little fear of retribution."[3] Florence Carman was on trial for murdering Louise Bailey because Florence had suspected her husband was habitually adulterous. Blanca must have heard echoes of her own marriage in the arguments and testimony. What did Blanca think when she first realized that wronged American wives had some sort of a right to commit murder?

We can speculate about the degree to which Blanca consciously copied Mrs. Carman's crime. Blanca de Saulles hired the same law firm that successfully defended Mrs. Carman. She retained Henry A. Uterhart, already famous for saving attractive ladies from the consequences of their conduct. Uterhart referred to Blanca as a "girl," portraying his client as the true victim, as broke, misused, and abused by the very man she shot. "He married her for her money," Uterhart said, "grew cold toward her when her fortune did not come up to his expectations, got $47,000 of her fortune of $100,000 by deception, became unfaithful early in their married life, took women companions into their apartment, and took the boy out with them, treated her brutally and contemptuously in the presence of her son and servants, and tried to destroy the boy's affection for her."

Her trial began November 19, 1917, at the Old Mineola Courthouse on Long Island. She faced the sob sisters and an all-male jury of middle-aged men. Blanca wore childish clothes to accentuate her diminutive stature, including a white silk blouse with pearl buttons and patent leather shoes.

The jury first heard a firearms expert, Capt. William A. Jones, testify that Blanca's .32 Smith & Wesson had a safety lock, and she would have had to release the lock each time she fired. Several eyewitnesses to the murder also testified, firmly establishing beyond all doubt that somewhere under the schoolgirl outfit lurked the mark of Cain.

Then Blanca testified, and she was pale and beautiful. She caused a commotion before she even took the stand. The fashionably dressed women in attendance stampeded for seats. Three fainted. Several were hurt. The judge came out of chambers and yelled, "This is simply disgraceful," as he evicted them all.

Blanca testified her husband was a ruthless fortune hunter who was disappointed that his wife wasn't as rich as he thought, as well as an abusive drunk who had affairs. Some of the jurors wept at the description of her marriage. Through her testimony, her attorney also put forth a defense of "mental confusion" due to an old head injury, a defective thyroid, and the heat of August.

The prosecution challenged her with her own prior statements. After her arrest, she had proclaimed, "I shot my husband because he would not give me my boy, and I hope he dies." She claimed amnesia. The prosecution then brought up Florence Carman, the woman who had recently been tried for shooting her husband's alleged mistress. Blanca was asked if she attended that trial. Blanca admitted that she was present on the day that the critical prosecution witness—Mrs. Carman's maid—said under oath that Mrs. Carman confessed. Blanca further stated that she "heard that black thing testify."

Asked what she meant, she said, "a nigger."

Even then it was a shocking thing to say. Observers may have gasped together.

But it didn't matter. None of the evidence mattered. Said a woman observer, "She'll get off all right. Look how pretty she is."

"Not guilty" was the verdict.

One of the jurors told her, "We're your friends, little girl."

Said the judge, sincerely: "I hope you will be happy now."

Said the *New York Times* in a December 3 editorial: "It need not be pointed out that it is not the intention of the law that a person who takes the life of another shall go scot-free."

After the trial, Blanca posed for press photos. Then she admitted that her listless demeanor during the trial was a calculated ruse. "I schooled myself in repression," she admitted. "I knew every amateur psychologist and sob sister would be studying my features, my expressions and my every movement."

Said one headline: ANOTHER PRETTY WOMAN HAS BEEN ACQUITTED.

Blanca moved back to Chile, taking her son with her. There she wed again in 1921. That marriage failed as well. Upon his maturity, her son renounced her and moved back to the United States. Blanca committed suicide on March 21, 1940, at the age of forty-five, prematurely ending a life full of heartbreaks.

✢ ✢ ✢

On January 11, 1919, another spousal killing took place mere yards from where Jack de Saulles was gunned down by his ex-wife. This time, it was Jacques Lebaudy who was shot five times by Marie Augustine Lebaudy with a .32. The Lebaudy estate of thirty acres adjoined the de Saulles estate; the same patrolmen who arrested Mrs. de Saulles also arrested Mrs. Lebaudy. "Yes, I shot him,"

Mrs. LeBaudy as featured in the *Boston Evening Globe,* January 15, 1919. (Public domain, via Newspaperarchive.com.)

she admitted to the police. "He deserved it. But I will go free. Look at Mrs. Carman and Mrs. de Saulles." After hearing her testimony, a grand jury agreed, refusing to indict her. Murder begat murder begat murder.

PAULINE
DUBUISSON

THE VICTIM: Félix Bailly
WHEN: March 17, 1951
WHERE: Paris, France
DEFENSE COUNSEL: Paul Baudet

THE CASE

Pauline Dubuisson, twenty-six, committed a *crime passionel* that elec-
trified all of Paris and indeed the world for three trial days in 1953
and tested the French resolve to treat such matters as entirely private.
Women particularly, rich and poor alike, flocked to the story of the
femme fatale who would come to be known as "Pauline the Perverse."

Pauline was accused of the cold-blooded murder of her former lover
out of spite because he loved another. The trial that followed was the
most exciting Paris had seen in years, and the entire city relished every
morsel of evidence as fast as the presses could print the statements of
witnesses and the delicious details of an attractive woman's active love
life. Her prosecutor would call her "a lioness; the most perverse criminal I have encountered in my career." Newspapers across the globe covered the case in depth, tracing the origins of the woman on trial for her
sexual escapades as much as her fatal assault on Félix Bailly.

The trial, and thus the reporting, dwelled on Pauline's romantic adventures, which began by the age of fourteen. She grew up in German-
occupied Dunkirk, France, and made herself well known for consorting
with Nazi sailors and officers. It was said Pauline kept lists of her lovers

along with notes regarding their styles of lovemaking with ratings of each in a little black book. This bit of her biography conjured the ancient legends of the fatal beauty who takes on the role of the enemy's sexual companion, which Pauline Dubuisson did quite literally. Upon the liberation of France, she and others like her were rounded up and publicly humiliated for their wartime proclivities. She was stripped in public, her head shaved, and according to lore, her influential father barely saved her from the firing squad.

Yet from this low beginning she was able to rebuild her life. She furthered her education at university, where it was later said she took many lovers from the faculty of the institution. She met Félix Bailly, a fellow student, at a medical school in Lille, and they were together for three stormy years. It was said she had other lovers during this time and rebuffed her boyfriend's proposal. Eventually the marriage-minded Félix met a woman in Paris whom he adored and became engaged to her. Said Pauline, "It was then that I realized that I loved him." Pauline demanded he break things off with his fiancée. He refused. Pauline, angered by his rebuff, decided to kill him and then herself. She wrote a will and made other preparations and then shot and killed Félix Bailly.[1]

After murdering him, she tried to kill herself with gas, but she was found and roused before the fatal last breath. Upon her arrest, her father succeeded in killing himself by the same method.

While awaiting trial in a Parisian jail, Pauline tried to kill herself by slashing a wrist. She had left a suicide note saying she preferred death over facing a public "who had not changed since the howling mob of the Revolution."

Initially, it seemed the great public furor her case aroused boded well for Pauline, and her demeanor evidence was the best a femme fatale could offer. The *Odessa Texas American* was among the countless newspapers across the world to broadcast a careful description of the woman accused of murder: "Pauline, throughout her trial, maintained calm. A slender, intelligent-looking girl, she had a wealth of curly chestnut hair framing a deathly pale face and somber eyes framed in long dark lashes. She wore a plain navy suit, white blouse open at the neck. There was nothing sensational about her, but everyone was conscious of her charm and sex appeal."

Her brilliant attorney had enough to work with to weave a tale of woe for the eleven men and one woman on the jury. His closing speech for the pretty accused killer was widely reported as a model of its kind. "In deathly silence the public listened to the impassioned plea for mercy of the girl's counsel, Maitre Baudet, which brought tears to the eyes of the public," the wire services reported. "Even the two hefty gendarmes sitting on either side of the prisoner appeared moved."

Regardless, Pauline could not completely hide the more perverse side of her nature, and the public prosecutor was merciless in pointing out the less flattering facts of the case. Glimpses of her sordid thoughts and habits were to be found in the mountain of evidence against her. The prosecution's closing argument was devastating to Pauline. The prosecutor, M. Raymond Lindon, noted that three weeks before the fatal shooting, Pauline Dubuisson had drawn up a will in favor of a woman named Colette Bigot. "Who is that woman Bigot?" asked the prosecutor. "She is a woman who was condemned to forced labor for life in this very court for murdering her two children within several years and who simulated suicide on each occasion.

"She didn't leave her money to her mother," he continued. "No, Pauline Dubuisson left her money to the most inhuman mother who ever walked this earth. There is a secret and monstrous harmony between the two crimes."

The jury returned in under an hour and disappointed Pauline, finding her guilty. She heaved a heavy sigh and smiled sadly. Later, she was condemned to life imprisonment for murder.

That of course was for show. She served six years and was out not long after turning thirty. They may well have shortened her life by letting her go. Released on parole, Pauline moved to Morocco to work in a hospital. She soon fell in love again. When she was jilted in 1963, she decided once again to end her life. Pauline finally killed herself with an overdose of sleeping pills.[2]

✝ ✝ ✝

For more information: Brigitte Bardot played a role based on Pauline Dubuisson in filmmaker Henri-Georges Clouzot's *La Verité* (*The Truth*) (1960).

PRINCESS FAHMY

THE VICTIM: Ali Kemel Fahmy Bey

WHEN: July 10, 1923

WHERE: The Savoy Hotel, London, England

DEFENSE COUNSEL: Sir Henry Curtis-Bennett and Sir Edward
Marshall Hall

THE CASE

At a hotel *de luxe* in London on a stormy summer night in 1923, a porter
named John-Paul Beattie heard an argument. The prince and princess
were at it again—screaming at one another in the corridor.

The porter interjected himself in their argument and politely begged
them to return to their suite. But as he walked away, he heard three
gunshots. He turned back and saw a horrifying sight. The millionaire
prince was lying on the carpet, blood gushing from the back of his head.
He had just been killed at twenty-two for no reason by his wife.

The princess dropped a hot Browning .32 and cried out many times
in French, "What shall I do? I've shot him!" She cradled his head in her
lap and repeated, "What have I done, my dear? I lost my head. We were
quarreling over the divorce. Oh, what have I done?"

The hotel manager arrived and, taking in the scene, turned to her
and asked, "Why have you done this terrible thing?"

Already her mind had turned away from the death she had just inflicted on a man who loved her and toward self-preservation. She replied in French, "Oh, sir! I have been married for six months, which has
been torture to me."[1]

Soon the whole world found itself asking the same questions: Who was this widow, why did she shoot her husband, and what ought to be done about it? To the cynical, there was only one question: She took his life; would she take his money too?

Marie (for simplicity's sake) was born into the Parisian working class in 1890. She gave birth to a daughter at sixteen. She then embarked on a life of high-end prostitution at the best cabarets and at Madame Denart's *maison de rendezvous.* Blessed with a fine figure, a dark complexion then much *en vogue,* and an exotic cast to her features, she became known as one of the most beautiful and well dressed of the Parisian experts in the romantic arts. Domination was the specialty of this *grande cocotte.*[2] She was photographed with a slender whip.

"Maggie Meller" (her working name) enjoyed high demand for her company when she met the young Prince of Wales in 1916. The future King Edward VIII was smitten with her. He spent much of the war visiting his famous mistress in Paris. After her dalliance with British royalty came to its natural conclusion, she blackmailed the prince with his indiscreet correspondence to her. Marie also made many other noteworthy conquests, eventually becoming a wealthy woman via divorce.

Then one day our heroine found herself in the Semiramis Hotel in Cairo, enjoying the attentions of a handsome young man. He was later introduced to her in Paris at the Hotel Majestic as a wealthy Egyptian prince. Like the British prince she knew before, the Egyptian millionaire was ten years her junior, twenty-two to her thirty-two, and he was mad for her. She was soon accompanying him on his international travels. He wrote her love letters extolling her "bewitching charm," which is the only explanation for his rash decision to ask for her much-admired hand in marriage—knowing full well that she was, to be harsh, perhaps, a notorious Parisian whore who slept with a pistol. Appalling his family, he wed her in late 1922.

The ridiculous marriage begun, his possessive jealousy and her ingrained flirtatiousness fueled ever-escalating fights, so they embarked on a dramatic married life consisting of, as the prince said to a friend, "the opera, theatre, disputes, high words and perverseness."[3]

One evening while out on the town they quarreled in public. She said to him in French, "You shut up, or I will smash this bottle over your head." Later in the evening, the leader of the band asked her if she had a request. Marie replied, "I don't want any music—my husband has threatened to kill me." Within twenty-four hours, it was her husband who lay facedown on the carpet with blood gushing from his gunshot wounds.

Two months after the mariticide, Madame Fahmy stood in the dock at the Old Bailey in London to answer for what she had done. The press was raving for details. The trial caused a sensation all over the world, particularly in Egypt, albeit an unpleasant one. Representing the state at her trial was Sir Percival Clarke (who would go on to try another femme fatale in the same courtroom—Elvira Barney). A jury that included two women were selected to hear the case. Marie chose a famous orator, Sir Edward Marshall Hall, to defend her name, such as it was (or should that be her *many* names), and slander her husband. The evidence against her began with reams of love letters from the prince to his bride. As they were read, the distressed defendant drooped against a wardress for support.

Famous weapons expert Robert Churchill took the witness stand to testify against a femme fatale for the first time in his career (the second being his testimony in the trial of Elvira Barney). Churchill testified that the gun that Princess Fahmy had used to kill her young husband could not have gone off accidentally as claimed.[4]

Defense counsel, playing to stereotypes, urged that despite the happy, romantic letters, the exotic prince had an evil side and was a "ferocious brute with a violent temper." Hints were made about the unnatural sexual tastes of this deceased foreigner.

But it was what Princess Fahmy had to say, and how she said it, that mattered most. Her second defense attorney, Sir Henry Curtis-Bennett, would later recall that she was "a calm, beautiful figure when she went into the witness-box." Through copious tears, the beautiful figure told of traveling to her husband's homeland. She told stories of life in a Cairo palace, a visit to the tomb of Tutankhamen that may have cursed them, moonlight voyages on a luxurious yacht, and the drama of a beautiful woman's terror. In the midst of Middle Eastern luxury, she sobbed, she made discoveries about her husband that filled her with loathing. Much was left to the imagination.

Then she told her tale of the fatal evening. They were talking about expense money and "he started tearing off my dress. He struggled with me. . . . I felt very frightened and very weak. He advanced with a very threatening expression, saying: 'I will revenge myself.' I took up the pistol. . . . Suddenly he brutally seized me by the throat, and with his right hand pressed me behind, saying: 'I will kill you now.' His thumb was on my windpipe, his fingers were round my neck. Stepping back, he said: 'I will kill you.' He tried to spring on me. I put my arm in front of me and as he was about to spring on me I lifted my arm without looking." That is all she could remember before she found her husband dead.

After just an hour of reflection on this account (which was entirely contradicted by the ballistics evidence and the testimony of the hotel porter who was present), the jury accepted it and pronounced a not guilty verdict.

Cheering broke out for the acquitted murderess. The judge, who bore the ironic name of Mr. Justice Swift, had the final say:

"Let her go."

LAURA FAIR

THE VICTIM: Alexander Parker Crittenden
WHEN: November 3, 1870
WHERE: San Francisco, California
DEFENSE COUNSEL: Elisha Cook

THE CASE

Prominent trial lawyer Alexander Parker Crittenden, fifty-eight, of the prominent Kentucky Crittendens, along with his wife, sons, and daughter, was on the crowded ferryboat *El Capitan* crossing the San Francisco Bay when a heavily veiled woman approached and pulled a gun. Before the horrified family, she shot the lawyer in the heart. He slumped against his wife and slid to the deck.

The woman dropped the pistol and then entered the main cabin area of the ferry, attempting to mingle with the other passengers. She was seized.

The victim's son, Parker Crittenden, cried out, "This is the woman! I accuse her of the murder of my father! Arrest her!"

She confessed at once. "I do not deny it. I did it. He ruined me and my child."

The killer was the victim's doxy, thirty-five-year-old Laura Fair. She had long ago declared that the day would come when she would see him one last time—never to part, or to part forever. She committed the murder out of jealousy, but she would later make the amazing claim that she was "unconscious" at the time.

What followed was a close examination of a woman of "great personal beauty," according to the official report of the case.[1] Laura first married at sixteen to a man named Stone, but she was widowed within a year. She then married Thomas Grayson, but they were soon divorced. With her mother and sister, she moved to San Francisco. It was said she taught music, and this is how she met Col. William D. Fair. Their marriage, too, was doomed, as he committed suicide. Along the way she had a girl, said to be beautiful little thing. Laura Fair and kin roamed around the west. She kept a boardinghouse in Sacramento, appeared on the stage in several coastal towns, and finally opened lodgings in Virginia City, Nevada, upon the discovery of silver. There, in the fall of 1863, she met and fell madly in love with Alex Crittenden.[2] She would soon need his professional services. Laura got in an argument with her business partner over whether to hang a flag above their establishment. During the dispute, Laura shot and wounded her partner. Crittenden would represent her in the trial on the charge. It was said the jury acquitted her without even leaving the box to deliberate.

A year after they met, she learned her lover had a wife and children back East. Yet the affair with Crittenden continued for years, memorialized in copious correspondence between them. More than a hundred love letters would one day become exhibits. On those grounds, her attorney Elisha Cook declared that "no two living beings on the face of God's footstool ever cherished for each other greater, more sincere, or deeper love than these two did." One of Crittenden's many letters to Laura read in part:

> No—I *can not*—*cannot* be content. You are to me sun—air—life—everything; and without you—as we now are—there can be no existence. I am wretched; insufferably, infinitely wretched; have no mind or heart for anything—can think of nothing but you. Day and night I wander about like a restless ghost. It is vain to tell me to be content.
>
> A. P. C.

It seems Crittenden had kept Laura Fair enthralled for years, in part by making promises to divorce his wife. When he failed to keep them, Laura impulsively married one Jesse Snyder in 1870. They were divorced within weeks. She returned to Alexander and was intimate with him from then on, the trial report notes, "up to within an hour before the killing."

When her trial finally began, authorities posted policemen to keep out the public. Only attorneys and reporters were permitted to attend. Prosecutors would prove at her trial that Laura Fair had made threats of bloodshed toward Crittenden in the past; she told a friend that one of the three of them in the love triangle would have to die; she bought the gun just a few days before the shooting; she engaged a boatman the day before the shooting to take her to the ferry, wait for her, and take her away from it; and she wore a disguise. The circumstantial evidence of premeditation was overwhelming.

Laura Fair had to testify. Rather than appearing to be acutely mentally ill, she appeared to be a woman ahead of her time. The officials recording the trial noted that from the dock, she "exhibited wonderful self-possession, ability, determination and nerve." In the eyes of Victorian men sitting on a jury, that would not sit well at all. A much-married, part-time actress who traveled widely and ran boardinghouses was suspected on all four counts of unsexing herself. She should have fainted.

The jury convicted her of first-degree murder.

The judge sentenced her to hang.

The public recoiled.

The verdict of guilty was one thing, but few had the stomach to execute a woman, let alone an attractive woman. The editors of the *San Francisco Examiner* were among those who decried Laura's death sentence: "No man who reverences the memory of a mother can contemplate with other feelings than horror, the hanging of a woman."[3]

The appellate courts would not hear of it. The verdict was thrown out on appeal, the higher court citing as error the introduction of evidence that Fair's "reputation for chastity" was not good. In a second trial, the jury rendered the more palatable verdict of not guilty by reason of insanity. Regardless of the verbiage, the killer was turned loose.

After her release, Laura Fair left the public eye; aside from publishing her memoirs,[4] she vanished into an obscure retirement until her death in 1919. Apparently four marriages, two shootings, one murder, and two trials were drama enough for this femme fatale.

ANNIE GEORGE

THE VICTIM: George DeWalt Saxton

WHEN: October 7, 1898

WHERE: Canton, Ohio

DEFENSE COUNSEL: John Cullen Welty and James Sterling

THE CASE

Ohio governor William McKinley was elected to the United States presidency in 1896, making Ida Saxton McKinley the First Lady of the United States, which is why on a cool autumn evening two years later, the discovery of the murdered corpse of her notorious brother George Saxton was an acute embarrassment for the White House. President McKinley immediately knew who was responsible—"*that* woman!" Everyone knew his meaning.

The president immediately traveled to Ohio for his brother-in-law's funeral, taking the attention of the nation with him. As the McKinleys feared, the murder made headlines everywhere. The scandal could not be contained. The First Lady's family would forever be known for supplying the corpse in what would become "the best Ohio murder of the 19th century."[1]

Years before the fatal night, George Saxton was a well-known local lothario with a string of broken engagements behind him when he was struck dumb at the first sight of Annie George shopping in a hardware store. She was a tall, pretty lady with a figure to envy. He decided to pursue her, even though she was married to Sample George. It was later said it took him two full years to seduce Mrs. George, and even then, it did not happen until her husband worked all winter far from home. The affair had predictable consequences for Mrs. George's marriage, which came to an unnatural end in a courthouse in the quickie divorce capital of South Dakota, but not before her husband sued the playboy for alienating her affections, assuring newspaper coverage of the scandal. Every detail of the case was printed in newspapers throughout Ohio, from the attorneys involved to the facts of the case to the legal theories presented. The Georges and Mr. Saxton all became locally famous for the "heart balm" litigation.

Annie would later insist that she left her husband and sons to take up with George Saxton because he promised to marry her. If he did, he breached his promise, just as he had done to other women, discarding her with cruel words and leaving her alone, fallen, and destitute. She ended her marriage for him, and he had left her without her husband, a home, a family, or any means of support.

Annie was devastated, her life destroyed, and in her ruin she became what we today call a stalker. She harassed George Saxton day and night, especially when she spotted him with other women, advising them against him because he had wrecked her life. She persisted in this even after Saxton obtained a restraining order against her. She persisted even when George found a steady paramour who was not dissuaded by harassment. Annie daily confronted them as they traveled the streets of Canton. This went on for years, their interactions becoming more virulent as their hatred for one another grew.

Annie George was regularly heard making remarks about George Saxton, such as, "If George Saxton does not keep his promise of marriage to me, I'll kill him, damn him, I'll kill him!"

"There will be a wedding or a funeral," she was heard saying.

"I will shoot him so full of lead that he will stand stiff," she threatened.

"If he fails to keep that promise I will kill him," Annie told an acquaintance. "I'll do it if I hang the next day, but I do not think any jury on earth would convict me after hearing my story."

The entire town was waiting for the other shoe to fall, so when the night came that four or five shots rang out in the streets of Canton, Ohio, the first thought of many was, "Saxton is getting it!" He did, fatally. They found his body on the steps leading to the home of Mrs. Eva Althouse, a Canton widow.

Annie was well attired for her acquittal. She wore "a crowd-pleasing outfit featuring a white waist with purple stripes and a white sailor hat with a black band and jaunty turkey feather." Many trial observers openly stared at her, "entranced by the attractive defendant."

In his closing remarks for her, attorney James Sterling called the victim everything but a child of God, responsible for the ruin not only of Mrs. George but of her husband and children. "He was a deliberate, designing libertine and seducer," Annie's attorney said. "I say that the air is purer by his passing away, and our wives, sisters and daughters are safer because of his spirit taking its flight. Like a serpent, he placed his vile arms around the wife of Sample George's youth. He gratified his lust, then drove her from his presence. He persecuted her. He had no thanks, no pity for the loss of her home, her happiness, her life. There are worse crimes than murder. . . . The life that George D. Saxton led had but one end—and that end was in blood. Who knows how many outraged hearts there were who were wishing for the death of Saxton? Who knows that some revenge-seeking person slew him, knowing that when he died that blame would be placed upon the prisoner?"

When the jury announced its verdict of not guilty, the courtroom erupted in what the press would call a "wonderful exhibition of joy" that spilled into the streets and lasted several hours.

Some attributed the verdict to Populist sentiment in favor of the working-class woman who was cruelly used by a member of the ruling class, the brother-in-law of the president of the United States.

Not all present were joyful, of course. Said prosecutor Atlee Pomerene to two physicians seated in the courtroom, "Which of you doctors was it that performed the criminal operation on the goddess of justice that resulted in this miscarriage?"

After having some time to cool off, the prosecutor added, "The verdict can have only one effect, and that is to lower the standard of public morality, of regard for law and order." The *New York Times* agreed, pointing out that the victim of the crime was afforded no chance to state his side of the case. After all, George Saxton could have told an equally compelling story of a mentally unbalanced woman who made his life a living hell for years. But Saxton never got to tell his story. "His slayer took care that he did not," the *Times* stated. "There is no more helpless thing than a dead man. A live woman has far more power. The acquittal of 'Mrs. George' is a hint to certain kinds of women how to proceed when they allow the spirit of murder to take possession of them."

Annie George's defense attorney, John Cullen Welty, took the opposite view of the verdict's potential impact upon society. "I hope it will have the effect of making the adulterer more cautious in his career of vice," Welty said. "It should mean, and I hope it will mean, the elevation of woman to her proper place in the home."

Speaking for herself, Annie George made an effort to be magnanimous. "Pleased with the verdict and with my treatment in court? Indeed I am," she said. "God only knows or ever can know, what I have suffered during the last eleven years of my life. I have been through temptation, darkness, persecution and even the shadow of death. I have suffered more than a thousand deaths, and many, many times would I have gladly laid down in the grave. But now the darkness is over and I shall forgive my enemies and persecutors and am fully resolved to live an upright life."

For a brief time, Annie George attempted to capitalize on her infamy by taking to the lecture circuit. She offered to speak at various establishments, but the reaction was swift. Prior to her scheduled speech in Xenia, Ohio, the ministers of that city issued a joint protest against her appearance, begging the women of Xenia, "in the name of Christian womanhood, the sanctity of the home, the sacredness of motherhood and pure morals to refrain from encouraging this shameless flaunting of a confessedly wicked life in the faces of good people."

The various reactions to the verdict in *Ohio v. George* speak to the complexity of the issues and emotions that arise when a woman steps down from the proverbial pedestal and commits a brutal act of revenge against a man. That a femme fatale aroused the sympathies of the common man on the street as well as in the jury room speaks to the plight and powerlessness of a woman abandoned by her lover in the Midwest at the turn of the century. By murdering him, Annie George arguably enforced the moral order of Ohio. Her overwhelming desire was not to kill George Saxton but to marry him, according to her many statements before the murder. Failing that, she killed him. For twelve male jurors, it was an understandable and excusable backlash against the victim's apparent transgressions. George Saxton's bloody murder would be officially traced to his character flaws.

Annie George resumed her life in Canton and married again.

President McKinley, like his brother-in-law, would come to an untimely end. McKinley was fatally shot by an anarchist in 1901. The president's assassin—being male—was executed within weeks of committing his ghastly crime.

CLARA SMITH HAMON

THE VICTIM: Jacob "Jake" Hamon
WHEN: November 21, 1920
WHERE: Randol Hotel, Ardmore, Oklahoma
DEFENSE COUNSEL: Jimmy Mathers

THE CASE

"Stunning beauty" is how the chief of police would remember the young Clara Smith.

"A little girl," her attorney described her. "Wouldn't weigh over one hundred pounds soaking wet—but she had brains and fire and drive."

"A modern vampire," said another attorney familiar with the facts of her life.[1]

Still a teenager, the petite stunner was working a counter at a dry goods store in Lawton, Oklahoma, in 1910 when in walked a millionaire twice her age. Jake Hamon, an attorney turned into a city attorney turned into the mayor of Lawton, was an oil magnate who made large political donations. He served as national Republican committeeman and had political hopes for himself.

He certainly should have known better. But one thing led to the next, and Jake Hamon made the counter girl an offer she gladly accepted. Miss Smith was packed off to business school and then finishing school and represented to the world as Jake's "secretary." He escorted her on whirlwind tours of the oil fields and boomtowns for what she called "a few short hectic years—a roseate dream of bliss"—or was it a gilded trap of vice, as she would later claim?—before complications beset the May-October romance: his wife Georgia and their son and daughter.

He first tried to solve the problem by wedding his mistress to his idiot nephew, a marriage of convenience that made her Clara Smith Hamon. Then he packed his family off to Chicago. On November 2, 1920, however, Ohio Republican senator Warren G. Harding was elected president of the United States in a landslide. Jake Hamon suddenly had a chance to make a political debut. There was talk of his nomination to a cabinet post as secretary of the interior. He made plans to move to Washington, DC. But he would have to take his wife and children; there was no more room in his life for his "secretary."[2]

Three weeks later, on Sunday, November 21, a gun went off in the Randol Hotel. Jake Hamon, gutshot, stumbled from his rooms. Surgeons removed the bullet and pressed the wounded man for an explanation. Jake claimed he accidentally shot himself, which no one believed. Days later, he was dead.

Clara was eventually tracked by Universal Wire Services reporter Sam Blair to a village in Mexico; she surrendered to authorities. In short order, she used her connections to amass a flock of lawyers, headed by James "Jimmy" Mathers, an Ardmore trial legend who knew and detested Jake Hamon. At twenty-eight, Clara faced ten days of proceedings in which she and her attorneys waged war on the dead man's character. She offered a diary in which she played the long-suffering victim to Jack's brutishness. Her lawyers portrayed the shooting as a tragic accident. During the trial, Clara received several Hollywood offers. The jury was out for less than an hour before acquitting her. The courtroom spectators cheered in unison, heartily approving a verdict that officially left the death of Jake Hamon "unsolved." The trial itself would become the stuff of legend in Oklahoma, studied by lawyers, judges, historians, and students of the curious ever since.

But the trial could not quench that particular thirst for notoriety that seizes some women. Like many femmes fatales before and since, Clara allowed the adulation of the court crowd and the verdict of the jury to persuade her that the keen public interest in her would outlast the proceedings. Within a week of her acquittal, Clara was off to Hollywood.

Clara thought she was famous when in reality she was infamous. Her first movie was marketed as autobiographical and titled *Fate*.[3] It was as one-sided as an apple pie. A nationwide backlash followed that ended Clara's movie career. At the premiere in San Francisco, the producer was arrested for exhibiting a film that was offensive to common decency. The state of New York banned the picture entirely on the grounds that making a star of a murderess would "corrupt morals or incite to crime." Objections were heard to a femme fatale monetizing her immorality, her criminality, her infamy. A good many in the movie industry simply did not want to inspire more bloodshed—a realistic concern, as anyone from Chicago could attest.[4]

The resourceful Clara made the most of her one foray into acting. She married her director.

ALICE HARTLEY

THE VICTIM: Murray D. Foley
WHEN: July 26, 1894
WHERE: Reno, Nevada

THE CASE

In 1894, the Bank of Nevada building in Reno was a three-story affair. On the first floor presided the wealthy president of the bank, Murray D. Foley, forty-four, a former state senator and one of Reno's leading citizens. The second floor held medical and law offices. On the third, where the rent was cheapest, resided one Alice Maud Hartley, a beautiful portrait painter. On a late afternoon in July of that year, Reno's businessmen found the normal bustle of commerce interrupted by a pair of gunshots from inside the bank building.

A lawyer and a doctor tentatively stuck their heads outside their office doors and were stunned to see the banker, Murray Foley, staggering down the stairs from the top floor with a gunshot wound in his chest. The medical man led the wounded banker into his office as the latter stated the obvious: "Doctor, I am shot and am a dead man." This became true almost immediately.

In the meantime, the lawyer looked to the staircase, and he saw Miss Hartley, the small, brown-haired, gray-eyed, thirty-year-old artist, standing on the landing with a pistol in her hand. Advancing toward the lawyer, she demanded that he summon the police.

When the uniformed man appeared, Miss Hartley said, "I believe you are the sheriff," and she handed him her gun. "I surrender as your prisoner."

The sheriff obliged her, though the jail had no cells for women; Miss Hartley was locked up in the courthouse and put under guard. At her arraignment, she was represented by the same lawyer who met her on the stairs. She confidently pleaded not guilty, declining to explain why she killed the banker, but it was apparent soon enough that she was to be a mother in the near future, and this was the first *clue* to the motive behind the fatal shooting.

Alice Hartley was put on trial for murder in September of that year in the Washoe County Court. The women of Reno were particularly interested in the story and packed the courtroom; many had already come to the conclusion that the married banker and the beautiful painter were secret sweethearts, her life had been wrecked by pending maternity, and it was the banker's fault.

Their assumptions found proof when Miss Hartley took the witness stand. She described an affair with the banker that made him appear to be a coercive ogre. "He frequently called on me," she said, "staying long past a reasonable hour. . . . he demanded that I drink brandy with him. . . . his expressions grew warm, causing me to grow fearful. . . . he stayed until daybreak . . . "—and so her story continued, herky-jerky.

Three hours later, the fact of their relationship was finally established as the spectators blushed and tittered and made other small noises. This scene was repeated for another five hours the following day until she finally reached the point of conception. At that time, she testified, she asked the banker to acknowledge the child to come. He stopped visiting. A quarrel followed on the fatal day, during which the banker struck her, she said, and denied the child; he said he would "buy some men with a few twenty-dollar pieces to testify to anything."

That's when she grabbed the pistol, and the rest was well known. But when it came time to describe the shooting, the defendant descended into hysterics, repeatedly fleeing the courtroom to be corralled in the hallway and returned to the stand.

The reaction to this pitiful tale was mixed in Reno. Many prominent women of the town took the lady's side in the matter, but others considered her a fallen woman, best convicted of her crime. One woman minister who visited and consoled her, Mila Tupper Maynard, was ostracized and had to leave Nevada. The all-male jury was sympathetic, but the facts and the law were clear. They convicted Miss Hartley of second-degree murder, recommending mercy.

For a moment, the defendant sat still. Then she stood and turned to the jury, saying, "Gentlemen, I thank you. I had hoped that you would exonerate me."

After her conviction, bail was granted, since nobody wanted to see a baby born in the courthouse. The convicted murderess had a boy, Vernon Harrison Hartley, and a few weeks later she received a sentence of eleven years in prison. After losing her appeal, she entered a women's penitentiary the next summer with her baby.

Almost immediately, an effort began to obtain her release, and the Pardon Board found itself ankle-deep in petitions for clemency. When one of these documents arrived containing the signatures of the very jurors who convicted her, the Parole Board relented. And after serving less than two years in prison, Miss Hartley and her little boy were released on the grounds that Murray Foley had wronged her, the shooting was justified, she had been punished enough, and she had a child to raise.

Alice Hartley promptly moved back to Reno and brought suit on behalf of her son against the Foley estate. The case dragged on in the courts, and at every hearing, the lively little baby was a prominent figure. But Miss Hartley's life again took a tragic twist when the baby died at the age of two from scarlet fever. She eventually lost the claim on the Foley estate and left Nevada for good.

Miss Hartley appeared in the newspapers on two more occasions before falling into obscurity. In 1897, she created a drama inside San Francisco's Emanuel Church. At the time, the city was rocked by a dramatic murder case involving one Durrant; the minister of the church preached about the case. Durrant had been convicted and sentenced to hang for the rape and murder of women inside the church. At the end of the sermon, Miss Hartley stood, and before the entire assembly, she declared that she had a message from God that Durrant was innocent, his life should be saved, and the congregation should make it a duty to see to this. Her speech was successful only in putting her on the front page again.

Her name appeared in the newspapers only one more time in 1899, when she married a San Francisco lawyer named William S. Bonnifield (who so happened to be the nephew of one of the Supreme Court justices who sat on the Pardon Board in Nevada and voted to grant her release). One has to wonder whether the wedding guests offered congratulations solely to the bride.

CLAUDINE LONGET

THE VICTIM: Vladimir "Spider" Sabich
WHEN: March 21, 1976
WHERE: Aspen, Colorado
DEFENSE COUNSEL: Charles V. Weedman

THE CASE

The trial of Claudine Longet for the murder of Vladimir "Spider" Sabich caused the press across the United States to go temporarily insane. Journalists from across the country converged on Aspen, Colorado, when Spider Sabich, a well-known Olympic skier, died at the hands of a world-class beauty, and they described for the rest of a shocked nation just who and what they found there.

In the 1970s, Aspen was internationally known for two things: world-class skiing and cocaine. It was "a hedonistic place where the rich, the young, the haunted and the newly divorced come to find a new sense of self," explained the *New York Times,* and Claudine Longet was all of those things. On March 21, 1976, she put Aspen on the map.

She was described in the press as a petite, curvy, attractive woman with dark hair and eyes and a brilliant smile. Claudine began her career in heartbreak as a dancer in a French revue in Las Vegas in 1961 where she met and married a singer, Andy Williams, who himself was about to become famous as the host of his own TV variety show that would enjoy a nine-year run and would feature his wife's singing ("You can tell when there's love in a home," she croons to Andy in one scene from the show).

They had a family together, producing three children, but not long after his show ended, they separated and eventually divorced.

That's when Claudine took up with Spider Sabich. Claudine and her three children moved into his Aspen mansion. Local legends abound concerning their stormy relationship. It was widely said that they were on the outs. Spider reportedly told a friend that "it's either going to end or we'll be married within a year." Sadly, the former became true within a month of his predicting it, and he was dead. Claudine called the police at once and to a detective she confessed, "I shot Spider."

As soon as she was released on bond, her ex-husband joined her to face the massed journalists together. As she awaited trial, she moved with her ex-husband and children into the Aspen mansion of famous singer John Denver, who had often appeared on Andy's show as well.

At her heavily attended trial, Claudine told a story that to this jaundiced eye is too ridiculous to quote at any length. Essentially, Claudine said that she and Spider were quite happy together and that his tragic death was an accident. She claimed that she was in the process of merely asking Spider how to use a gun when it just accidentally went off, mortally wounding him with one shot of a German-made .22 Irma pistol. That was her story, and the jury accepted this.

Colorado has a long tradition of acquitting femmes fatales; Claudine was the third, counting Grace Nottingham (sentenced to one day in jail in Colorado for shooting her boyfriend in 1903) and Gertrude Patterson (acquitted in Colorado of shooting her husband in 1911). The judge in Claudine's case also did her the favor of excluding some interesting evidence from her diary as well as the toxicology results that showed she was intoxicated when she committed the crime. Claudine, who was thirty-four at the time of her trial, played her part well. She wore the fashionable colors of a femme fatale on trial for murder, a knee-length fur coat over a black sweater over a white blouse with dark hose and black shoes—and a blue miniskirt, a nod to the times. She wept openly in court. Always the connoisseur of world-class femmes fatales, including so many women who played the part in innumerable films, actor Jack Nicholson attended the trial.

There is something about a beautiful woman's face that draws our attention, and something about that sort of attention that distorts the administration of justice for the victim and for society. Claudine Longet was found guilty of negligent homicide. The judge later sentenced her to thirty days in jail for killing her boyfriend.

She duly served her Colorado sentence.[1]

NELLIE MAY MADISON

THE VICTIM: Eric B. Madison
WHEN: March 24, 1934
WHERE: Burbank, California
DEFENSE COUNSEL: Joseph Ryan and Frank Ryan

THE CASE

Nellie May Madison shot her husband five times in the back and head while he was sleeping. This is not easy to explain, even for an attractive woman. The doctrine of self-defense has always required an "imminent" danger. When a beaten woman decides to get her man before he gets her, she often preemptively strikes while he is incapacitated. Unfortunately for Mrs. Madison, the law has always shaken a finger at slaying a sleeping drunk.

She was an unusual woman, and this was counted against her. Nellie May began her marital adventures at thirteen. She was married five times—this was when divorce rates were in the single digits. Despite all those husbands, she never had children. Then she bought a handgun and made herself a widow. Witnesses originally thought the gunshots came from the adjacent Warner Brothers studio.

Despite the Hollywood backdrop, Nellie May missed her cues. She had natural beauty going for her, but she played it all wrong. She did not contact the police after the killing; she fled and let her landlady find his body. The all-points bulletin told police to watch out for a "beautiful black-haired woman." The police found her two days later, hiding in a

A portrait of Nellie May Madison at the time of her trial in June 1934. (From the *Herald Examiner* Collection, Los Angeles Public Library.)

closet. She was stoic about her arrest. She did not weep into her handkerchief for a press pool waiting for a sob story. Indeed, she refused to say anything at all about the murder. An investigator called her "the coolest woman I have ever questioned in all my years." If she had a defense, she said nothing of it. Public opinion went against her. Reporters dubbed her "a real-life Roxie Hart," "a sphinx woman," a femme fatale. The prosecutor announced he would seek the death penalty.[1]

When she went on trial in the Hall of Justice in June 1934, Nellie retained attorney Joseph Ryan and his brother, Frank Ryan, to represent her. They tried to dismiss every woman who appeared for jury duty. Nellie's attorney said he thought male jurors would be "more sympathetic. After all, she's a woman, isn't she?" In the end, however, four women and eight men formed the panel. Curiously, her lawyer refused to put on the evidence that would explain why she did it. Attorney Joseph Ryan also declined to give an opening statement on behalf of Mrs. Madison. He proved to be an uninspiring cross-examiner. He never as-

Newspapers around the world published retouched images of Nellie May Madison. (From the *Herald Examiner* Collection, Los Angeles Public Library.)

serted self-defense as an excuse for the shooting death of Eric Madison. Instead, he argued that the dead man was not Eric Madison but some stranger who happened to die in his bedroom. The puzzled jurors contemplated the bloody, bullet-ridden bed set up in the courtroom, along with Nellie's icy, detached demeanor. They couldn't help but notice she wore the same black dress to court every day of the two-week trial. She may as well have pleaded guilty. The jury found her guilty of first-degree murder with a demand for the death penalty, and the judge sentenced her to the gallows. She was the third woman in California to ever receive the ultimate sentence.

Nellie Madison was imprisoned to await her hanging. The Supreme Court upheld her sentence, and the date was set for her to die. She fired her attorney and hired Lloyd Nix to handle her last-ditch legal efforts.

Finally, she confessed, admitting she blew her husband into eternity, claiming extenuating circumstances. Then she told a story of rib-cracking abuse to a sob sister—and the sob sister found proof. Former coworkers and employers described Eric Madison's foul and frightening rages.

Previous girlfriends and an ex-wife told virtually identical stories of stranglings, beatings, and humiliations that the flashpoint-tempered man heaped upon the many women in his shortened life. Though none of these stories had been subjected to cross-examination or any sort of scrutiny beyond an editor's eye, they saved Nellie's life. Under pressure from the public, the governor commuted her death sentence to life imprisonment with parole, and a parole board then reduced her time. Nine years to the day after the murder of her husband, and despite being sentenced to the rope, Nellie Madison was set free.

Whether Eric Madison had it coming or not, by golly he got it in spades.

JULIA MORRISON

People who are very beautiful make their own laws.
—Robert Allan Ackerman, director, *The Roman Spring of Mrs. Stone*

THE VICTIM: Frank Leiden
WHEN: September 22, 1899
WHERE: Backstage at the Chattanooga Opera House, Tennessee

THE CASE

The traveling play about to take stage at the Chattanooga Opera House was *Mr. Plaster of Paris,* a lighthearted comedy. Before the curtains went up, the waiting audience heard three shots ring out. *Part of the play?* they must have wondered. The first two pops went off in rapid succession; the third they heard after a slight delay. No one in the audience stirred until one of the actors came before the curtain with some terrible news about the lead actor. He was Frank Leiden, a fairly popular and well-known theater actor from New Orleans. Abruptly the audience was told, "There's been an accident. Frank Leiden has been killed." And indeed he was—shot dead in front of the whole cast and crew by his leading lady.[1]

It seems as the play was about to begin, Julia Morrison, a handsome blonde appearing in her first role, arrived at the very last minute, still in street dress and wearing no makeup. She marched into the theater with a .32 Smith & Wesson revolver in her hand, walked up to her co-star, and from a distance of three feet, right there in front of everyone, she shot him in the neck. She shot him again as he fell. While he lay bleeding to death, she shot him again in the face. Miss Morrison was immediately arrested and gave a long statement to the police admitting to the murder (it was undeniable), describing a series of bitter quarrels with her victim. He persecuted me, he insulted me, she declared; he tried to have my husband removed from the traveling show.

In 1900, Julia Morrison modeled for celebrity photographer Elmer Chickering. It was also the year the actress was acquitted by a Tennessee jury of the murder of her costar, whom she had shot at the Chattanooga Opera House. (Image courtesy Dr. David Shields.)

The State of Tennessee vs. Julia Morrison James was a production in three acts that played to a theater packed to suffocation. The crowds attending the sensational murder trial in Chattanooga in January 1900 crammed into the benches, crammed into the aisles, and even crammed themselves behind the judge's seat. The curtain lifted on Act I: The Prosecution.

The sympathy of the company was with the deceased. His only offense, they said, was in trying to get rid of her. She was an amateur who had gotten into the company by false pretenses, they reported. She was a "d— b—," said the assistant manager. One witness said he overheard the leading lady tell the leading man earlier in the day that "I will put a ball through you yet." Thus, the fact that a murder was committed was firmly established, with ample evidence of premeditation. Julia Morrison, if convicted, would hang.

But on to Act II and a life-or-death performance. The papers were careful to describe the defendant's appearance, her fluffy pompadour, her jaunty hat, her smiles and effusive greetings as the trial commenced. She took the witness stand with a confident air and proceeded to tell those assembled her sad life story. "She did not seem to realize the gravity of her situation," said the papers. Julia was orphaned as an infant and then raised by foster parents who subjected her to severe treatment, who sometimes beat her head against the wall, she said. She married before she was fourteen years old and worked as an office girl and a housekeeper before securing the leading role in *Mr. Plaster of Paris*. At first, she said, Frank Leiden was gentlemanly, telling her she was "great and excellent." Then, she said, he found out she was married. He was unkind thereafter, and she was forced to endure insults. On one occasion, he wrapped his arms around her and asked for a kiss and offered an indignity.

And he called her awful names. When told by counsel that she had to use the exact words of the "terrible oaths" he used against her, she sobbed for the first and only time during the trial. "Bitch" was among the epithets, but the papers couldn't print the rest. She also said he had a "violent temper" and once raised a cane to her, remarking, "You are not fit to act in an amateur company." And on another occasion: "You aren't fit to be in a dog show."

In the final act, Julia Morrison was punctually acquitted. She immediately rose and gave another speech, calling the jurors "just and generous."

She said, "Sitting there in the courtroom all day, how you long to rise and in a rush of recital tell of the tragedy of your existence, tell the degradation, the anguish, the horror, the brutality that has goaded you like red hot irons that burn slowly, slowly into the flesh every day with added intensity. Who are those twelve men, you want to cry, who dare to say if I am guilty or not?" She magnanimously forgave the prosecutors. Turning to the family of the man she killed, she said, "I leave them to their conscience and their God."

CHARLOTTE NASH NIXON-NIRDLINGER

> Gentlemen that marry beauty prize winners should behave themselves.
>
> —*Lincoln Star* on the Nixon-Nirdlinger verdict

THE VICTIM: Frederick C. Nixon-Nirdlinger
WHEN: March 11, 1931
WHERE: Nice, France

THE CASE

An aging millionaire, a beauty queen, a bottle of whiskey, a loaded pistol, an accusation of infidelity—put them all in one room and someone is bound to make headlines.

The story actually began eight years before that fateful booze-fueled night. It started the moment a pair of dimples framed by spun-gold hair strolled across a stage in Atlantic City, New Jersey, in the autumn of 1923. The sash draped across her teenage bosom identified her as "Miss St. Louis," though she usually answered to Charlotte Nash. She was seventeen years old, barely out of high school, and extremely pretty. Her one ambition was to become Miss America.

At least one of the judges thought her blue eyes and corn-fed cheeks warranted the title. He was Fred Nixon-Nirdlinger, world traveler and wealthy forty-seven-year-old owner of a chain of theaters in Philadelphia. But he was ultimately outvoted; the crown went to a young lady from Ohio. Nixon-Nirdlinger was furious and vowed that if he could not make Charlotte Nash into Miss America, then he would at least make her a famous actress. She was a "diamond of purest water," he said, just needing "a touch of polishing here and there."

Charlotte was trotted off to finishing school at Nixon-Nirdlinger's expense, where she learned the niceties of deportment; to rise, sit, and carry herself with dignity; and to soften her western *R*s. A few months into Charlotte's polishing regimen, Fred decided that his public, long-lasting search for "The One Woman" had finally come to an end. He withdrew her from the academy and married the eighteen-year-old beauty in a sensational ceremony in Hagerstown, Maryland. To a reporter, Fred said, "I find wives hard to keep—but I am going to hang on to this one until the end."

Alas, he neglected to tell his young bride the news. He was already married to someone else. In fact, he had been married for almost twenty years to Lura McKenna. He was also expecting a child by his mistress. The husband of a second mistress had just sued him for "alienation of affections" for playing the role of "the other man" in their divorce.

All these errors and omissions came to light while Charlotte and Fred were on a transatlantic voyage to their Paris honeymoon. Once she recovered from the dizzying bad news, Charlotte left him in Paris and returned to the United States.

Fred would not let his perfect woman get away. He nearly melted the cable lines begging her to return to him. Charlotte eventually caved in and put herself on a ship back to Paris. Quite the honeymoon followed. Jealous quarrels between bouts of lovemaking left Charlotte pregnant—and divorced.

They were hardly done with one another. After the child was born, Charlotte and Fred married again. Their second go-round was no better than the first. Fred, it seemed, was intensely jealous of his young and beautiful wife. According to the couple's friends, he hired detectives to follow her every move. The cycle of nasty confrontations between gentler interactions resulted in another child and a move to the French Riviera. It was in March 1931 that a certain villa on the Boulevard des Anglaise in Nice was the sight of a grisly tragedy, and Nixon-Nirdlinger became a household name.

The sole survivor of the disaster would later give an account of the fatal evening. Fred was drinking. Charlotte was seated, studying Italian. Fred asked her what she was doing and from her answer he surmised that Charlotte must be interested in an Italian fellow, and he said so. She denied this. He accused her of trafficking with gigolos. She denied this. The ensuing argument lasted for hours, turning ugly, resulting in Fred wrapping his hands around Charlotte's throat and threatening to choke her to death.

At some point Fred went into the kitchen for more whiskey. Charlotte used the opportunity to flee to the bedroom, where she slipped a loaded pistol under her pillow. Fred's last words to her were, "I will kill you rather than let you have an Italian lover." Charlotte beat him to it. As she lay on the bed, she retrieved her pistol and fired. The first bullet entered Fred's body just under his left eye and lodged at the base of his skull. A second bullet hit him in the chest. Two more shots went wild. Fred crumpled in a pool of blood.

Charlotte stood, dropped her pearl-handled pistol, and slipped in her husband's blood. Picking herself up, she stumbled into the hall, her arms and nightgown streaked with blood. She ran downstairs for the janitor, crying, "I have killed my husband." Then she fainted.

Charlotte Nixon-Nirdlinger was arrested and held in a French jail. She relayed her story of the evening to the police. They noted vivid red marks on her throat that deepened to bruises and came to the conclusion that she had been severely handled as she claimed. This prompted prosecutors to hold her on a charge of "murder with excuse of provocation."

The shooting death of the famous American millionaire became an overnight news sensation. Journalists from across Europe and the United States tried to land an interview with the accused. A woman reporter with the United Press snuck into the jail cell to report: "She was a pitiful figure in the dark prison dress, deprived of powder and lipstick, and faced with the task of defending herself in a foreign court room." Her attorneys could have bailed her out of jail before her trial set to begin two months later, but they made a cynical decision. In an effort to build sympathy for the self-made widow, they let her remain in jail. It was important for her complexion. She needed to be as pale as plaster. Her life also depended on staying out of deep trouble. "Had she been at liberty," one of the journalists later explained, "she would have looked less wan and miserable, and the sympathies of the public would not have been so wholeheartedly with her." Photos from her pageant days and pictures of her children were widely circulated in the press.

The careful descriptions of her appearance continued when her trial began a little over a month later. The trial of la belle dame sans merci drew throngs who stared at the woman facing the guillotine. As Charlotte the Beautiful came to court, the reporters noted that "the cleverest *couturiers* and *modistes* in Paris had offered her the choice of a costume that would both enhance her stricken beauty and at the same time follow the lines of simplicity and grief. She had selected a modestly long black gown, with white touches at the throat and cuffs, and a black hat."[1]

A jury of businessmen was selected to hear from a variety of witnesses who told stories of the dead man's jealousy. The couple's French friends testified that the slain man was "insanely jealous," never letting her out alone, reading every letter she wrote or received. The fact that the deceased was Jewish was also whispered.

A critical witness was a Swedish nanny who contradicted the prosecutor's effort to paint Charlotte in scarlet colors. The nanny insisted that Charlotte was as pure as Caesar's wife. "Mrs. Nirdlinger never flirted and never had any love affairs," the nanny said. "I would have known it if she had."

Then the widow testified—between sobs and gasps. "He came into the bedroom and said such disgusting things to me that I cannot repeat them. I fired—I did not mean to kill him."

On cross-examination, Charlotte denied the prosecutor's accusations that she danced and flirted with other men. The judge asked her if she had an affair with a swimming instructor. She vehemently denied this. When all was said and done, the prosecutor came up with two pieces of evidence that she was a wandering wife. One was a photograph of her in a fashionable bathing suit. Two, he read from a letter Charlotte wrote to a friend in which the unhappy young lady said, "There are nothing but constant rows. But I'll be damned if I'll stay home and sit in a corner reading. I am still young. Maybe when I'm his age I'll do that."

But there was more evidence against her; there was the physical evidence. There was the fact that she bought her handgun two months before she shot her husband, clearly a sign that she planned for a scene. There was the fact that she shot four times and missed twice suggested to the prosecutor that she was not standing all that close to her husband as she claimed, and she was never in imminent danger of death.

Above: Jubilant headlines met the news from Nice, France, of the acquittal of an American beauty queen. (From the *Burlington [Iowa] Gazette,* May 20, 1931, via Newspaperarchive.com.)

Left: "Beauty acquitted in French court of slaying hubby." (From the *Hanover [Pennsylvania] Evening Sun,* May 20, 1931, via Newspaper archive.com.)

Her lawyers were adamant that she acted in self-defense. "It's a clear case," said her lead attorney. "The fact that my client bought two months ago the revolver with which she shot and killed her husband does not indicate premeditation. She simply purchased the weapon for use in case of extreme emergency to defend her life. How prudent this action was." Her lawyer summed up his closing argument by lightly resting his hand on Charlotte's shoulder and declaring to the jury that "she is too beautiful to be bad."

The jurors included seven bachelors. They acquitted her in nine minutes. The judge released her with a final admonition. Though the investigation of her morals had a favorable outcome for her, he said she was still to be chastised for being "flighty in your thoughts, too much occupied with pretty dresses and dancing."

Thus, Charlotte Nash Nixon-Nirdlinger was acquitted on charges of adultery—umm, murder. The spectators cheered in the courthouse

Charlotte's story was published in delicious detail for months after her murder trial. (From the July 25, 1931, *Hamilton [Ontario] Evening Journal*, via News paperarchive.com.)

square to see her restored to liberty. Charlotte, her attorney, and her mother were swept up in a crowd that chanted, "Vive la belle Americaine! C'est la justice! L'amour! L'amour!"

She may well have been better off to remain in France. The verdict was largely attributed, by the American newspapers at least, to French attitudes toward beautiful women and marriage in general. But she returned to St. Louis. There she learned that her husband's will left her nearly penniless. She tried to find acting jobs in Hollywood only to be snubbed, as Hollywood would have none of her. On the bright side, I have it on reliable authority that she stayed in the United States and reached the ripe old age of one hundred years.

Toward the end of her fame Charlotte would declare, "Sometimes I'm sorry that I was ever considered beautiful. It brought me more trouble than joy."

Presumably her husband had similar sentiments in his last moments.

GRACE V. NOTTINGHAM

PSYCHOLOGISTS ARE BAFFLED BY THE STRANGE
ATTRACTION WHICH DRAWS MEN TO WOMEN WHO
SHOOT

—Headline in the *Port Arthur News,* May 10, 1936

THE VICTIM: Edward Murphy
WHEN: June 29, 1903
WHERE: Minturn, Colorado
DEFENSE COUNSEL: John A. Ewing

THE CASE

Grace Nottingham, the daughter of a well-to-do early settler, was born
and raised in the mountains of Colorado. She was the favorite of her
family and one of the prettiest girls to ever grace the Western Slope.
Edward Murphy was a railroad brakeman who wooed and won fair
Grace. Apparently, he spoke too much of their romance to others. The
only other thing anyone remembered about him is the way that he died.

Grace and Edward had a quarrel. Not so serious to begin with, probably, just something about his friends. He said something she didn't
like, and she said something else, and before long they were both hot.
Grace accused her fiancé of "ruining" her. In that time and place, this
was a transgression she could not abide. She demanded that Edward
pay her a hundred dollars to compensate her for her damaged reputation. When he refused to pay her, the conversation boiled over, she
snatched a gun, and she shot her sweetheart dead.

While shootings in the wilds of Colorado were not uncommon then, this particular shooting by a woman of more than ordinary beauty created a sensation throughout the state, and she was put on trial at Red Cliff. Her attorney pleaded both temporary insanity and self-defense and begged for clemency. The all-male jury rejected these defenses, however, and convicted her of involuntary manslaughter. Appended to the ver-

Grace Nottingham (*left*) and her music teacher. (Courtesy of the Eagle County Historical Society and the Eagle Valley Library District.)

dict was a recommendation for mercy. The judge obliged. The Honorable Frank Owens sentenced Grace Nottingham to one day in the county jail and $700 in costs for killing her boyfriend in a fit of pique.

What would have happened to her if she had been old and ugly?

With the sentence served, Grace was once again turned loose on mankind. The next to catch her eye was Henry Adler, a good-looking, well-dressed, divorced businessman from Chicago in pursuit of fortune. He was well known for his proclivity for flirting with young girls. He was also twice her age, and Jewish to boot. Over the objections of her family, they eloped to Los Angeles.

Within weeks Grace packed her bags and returned to Colorado alone. Her marriage had quickly proved an unhappy one. She took a job as a clerk in a music store and secured a divorce, citing cruelty. The papers would say she starting living the "high life" as a divorcée and took up with the owner of a restaurant.

On March 5, 1908, two bodies were found inside the Waldorf Hotel in Denver. Henry Adler was discovered sitting in a chair, dead. His ex-wife, Grace Nottingham, was lying across his knees, also dead. He had killed her, then turned the pistol on himself. A note in his pocket proved that jealousy was his motive.

She had been shot through the heart.

MADALYNNE OBENCHAIN

THE VICTIM: John Belton Kennedy
WHEN: August 5, 1921
WHERE: Los Angeles, California
DEFENSE COUNSEL: Charles E. Erbstein

THE CASE

John Belton Kennedy was an insurance broker and a child of privilege, the son of a wealthy businessman. His father had given him a present of an exotically decorated little cabin in the woods not far from Los Angeles. On a hot August night, on the steps leading to his cabin, Belton Kennedy was shot and killed.[1]

His lady companion screamed until startled neighbors arrived. They found her hysterically crying over his bloody body. "I love him! What have they done to him! He is mine. He is dead." She stepped away from her dead lover and into the cold embrace of eternal infamy. To the deputies she would tell this tale: "Belton and I had words. He walked to the door. He stood there for a few moments, silently. And then—then the shot rang out and he fell. I rushed to the door. I saw two ragged men, running away. They were the men that shot him."[2] She was taken home for the night. Within a week, however, Madalynne Obenchain was infamous worldwide—a beautiful, educated, well-to-do young woman arrested for conspiracy to commit the premeditated murder of her lover.

The Kennedy murder inspired the police to declare, "Cherchez la femme!"[3] They investigated his girlfriend only to discover that all was

Photograph of Mada-
lynne Obenchain, 1922.
(DN-0074141, *Chicago
Daily News* negatives col-
lection, Chicago History
Museum.)

not well in their relationship. In fact, Madalynne was in a fantastic
rage. She had divorced her husband, an attorney, to be with Belton,
but Kennedy steadfastly turned down her proposals of marriage. His
family refused to bless the match, he told her. His father once said to
Belton, "I would rather see you dead than married to that woman."[4]
Madalynne had the last word on the subject, police theorized.

Arrested along with Madalynne was another of her lovers, Arthur
Cowbrey Burch. The prosecutor handling the case announced that Madalynne Obenchain had convinced Arthur to stalk Belton Kennedy for
days, eventually shooting him from ambush. The police had amassed a
wealth of corroborative evidence concerning a car Arthur Burch had
rented for the job.

No sooner was the deadly divorcée behind bars and awaiting trial
when another lover rushed to her aid, a handsome and accomplished
lawyer who until recently had been her husband, Ralph Obenchain. He
declared to the press that he was not bitter about the divorce: "She is

the one woman in the world for me." Later he added, "I believe she is innocent." With her ex-husband's guidance, she chose as her attorney a well-known courtroom pugilist from Chicago, Charles E. Erbstein, whom the prosecutor immediately dubbed a corrupt, damnable devil's advocate, a "trickster," and a "sheister."

News spread that Madalynne had received marriage proposals behind bars—indeed, two at once. Her ex-husband and her codefendant were among those who sought her hand in marriage as she awaited trial. Then the prosecutor fell in love with Madalynne himself, if legends are true, and he bowed out of the matter to let another prosecute the case.[5] The press marveled at all the men who flocked around *la femme sans coeur*. Said one reporter, "Cleopatra was a piker compared with this woman."[6]

Kennedy apparently foresaw his destiny; in his safe-deposit box were nearly a hundred letters from her. The prosecutor read many of them into evidence, as they tended to show that Madalynne was madly in love with Belton Kennedy, and he did not return her affections with the same vigor. Mindless of the fact that she had many other men wrapped around her little finger, she was obsessed with Belton's rejection of her.

But that was mere conjecture. Madalynne Obenchain was not only beautiful, she was the best-dressed accused murderess to ever grace a dock. She made grand entrances into the Superior Court for Los Angeles County. On one day, she was a "smiling, confident, rather dazzling figure in blue with a low-cut neck and a diaphanous gown." On another day, she wore taffeta. The next, black fur with a rosebud. On another, long black gloves. And she stuck to her story.

The jury was hung. A second jury was hung. A third was hung. The newspapers ran out of amazement. A fourth, and so on, until the district attorney racked up an amazing record of five straight hung juries. Finally calling to an end the horrifying mockery of justice that the case had become, the prosecutor dropped all the charges. Belton Kennedy's death would not be avenged. By then, however, Madalynne Obenchain was convicted in the press—as guilty as a Medea, and equally unpunished.

BEATRICE PACE

> In many unsolved murder mysteries, the true difficulty which
> has confronted the police is not that of finding the criminal, but
> that of proving his guilt in a way which will convince a jury.
> —Scotland Yard Chief Inspector George Cornish

THE VICTIM: Harry Pace
WHEN: January 10, 1928
WHERE: The Forest of Dean, England
DEFENSE COUNSEL: Norman Birkett

THE CASE

Beatrice Martin was a country girl who went into service in London for three years, which she would later say were the happiest years of her life. She returned to the country and at nineteen years of age married a local sheep farmer, Harry Pace.

Eighteen years and ten children later, Harry fell quite ill. A terrible sickness in his stomach kept him in bed for weeks. He stumped his doctors with a curious collection of symptoms, including constant vomiting and paralysis in the limbs as weeks became months. Hospitalized for a time, he improved enough for discharge, but upon returning home he relapsed and finally died in agony. He was thirty-six.

His parents and siblings immediately suspected the worst. At their instigation, authorities conducted a postmortem examination of the farmer's body only to discover that he was full of arsenic. Local police called on Scotland Yard to investigate the "Fetter Hill mystery." After questioning everyone they could, the inspectors concluded there were two possible explanations for the premature death of Harry Pace: either Harry had committed suicide with arsenic or he was murdered with the stuff.

The suicide theory was quickly abandoned since the decedent had been ill for months all told, and such a slow and painful death was inconsistent with an impulse for self-destruction. The suicide theory was stupid. It made no psychological sense.

The murder theory had them aiming their sights at the dead man's widow, Beatrice Pace. Her in-laws could not disguise their loathing for her, accusing her of treating her husband poorly and running around on him. Mrs. Pace herself had informed the police that she and she alone gave her husband food and medicine in his final illness. Those who could avoid overthinking the matter came to the conclusion that Beatrice Pace had the exclusive opportunity to poison her husband. The next logical inference is it was more likely than not that she poisoned him.

The reading public took a different view of the case entirely. The press literally painted a pretty picture of the accused murderess with her "pretty bright eyes" and her "slender figure." The newspapers of the time "emphasized Beatrice's attractiveness," observed a scholar of the case.[1] The press published numerous photographs of the accused killer as well as photographs of the five surviving Pace children, who ranged in age from infancy to seventeen. The public would learn that the Paces had buried five of their offspring who had died in childhood, which was seen as the great tragedy of her life. "Year in and year out I had babies," Beatrice later recalled. "I would hardly have one old enough to sit up, when there was another in my arms." Today we are perhaps more cynical. If Beatrice Pace's case had arisen much later in the twentieth century, investigators might have requested, and might even have received, permission to exhume the bodies of Beatrice's deceased children to look for arsenic.

But in the 1920s, the newspapers portrayed Beatrice's suffering as a mother in moving detail and dwelled on her attractive figure and features, transforming a farmer's wife into a heroine, as odd a choice as she was for the role. "It is not unprecedented for the press to portray an accused murderer positively," points out historian John Carter Wood. "Press and public reactions to accused (and even convicted) killers were often unpredictable, sometimes surprising and occasionally mercurial. Those who killed for base motives, such as material gain, or whose acts were especially grisly were, unsurprisingly, vilified. However, killings committed in the heat of passion, in response to serious provocations or victimization or as a result of insanity might be treated with a striking degree of understanding."

Beatrice Pace understood this. In one of her many statements to police, Mrs. Pace gave accounts of abuse by her foul-tempered husband. Here she had to walk a fine line. She portrayed her husband as an ogre, simultaneously justifying killing him while claiming he killed himself. The press published her accusations against her husband, some of which was corroborated by the sworn statements of her older children.

Beatrice Pace described a nightmarish marriage in which Harry Pace had beaten her many times, threatened to kill her many times, and on occasion menaced her with weapons such as guns, a razor, and a hatchet. Twice he had killed a family dog by bashing its brains out. He had rages in which he would break things. Before he died, he threw a tantrum on Christmas Day and threatened to kill the entire family. Her children recalled this incident as well. Beatrice went further, even recounting having to pay the families of girls that her husband had raped, posthumously accusing her husband of child molestation.

Although much was said against the victim of the tragedy, who was unable to speak for himself, much could be said against fair Beatrice Pace and that she admitted. The public would learn of Beatrice's affairs outside her marriage but would never learn the details; nor were they told that she had taken an abortifacient to end an unwanted pregnancy at least three times. These details were glossed over or never appeared in the papers, as the press was united and unwavering in its support for the widow. By the time *Rex v. Pace* was gaveled into order in July 1928 at the Shire Hall in Gloucester, England, Beatrice Annie Pace "had a nation behind her."[2] The throngs, in which women outnumbered men, came by the thousands, surrounding the courthouse to catch a glimpse of the defendant on her way from jail to court.

The prosecution's case was simple: Harry Pace died of arsenic poisoning, receiving a massive final dose within two days of his death, and whatever was given him during that time, be it food, drink, or medicine, Mrs. Pace and only Mrs. Pace prepared it and served it. She had a supply of arsenic that was used as an insecticidal sheep dip on the sheep farm, and some of the arsenic seen by others was noted to be missing after Mr. Pace died. The circumstantial evidence pointed to one person to the exclusion of all others.

The prosecution may have made its singular mistake in putting much of this evidence into the record by calling on the relatives of the dead man. Beatrice's attorney, Norman Birkett, skewered Harry Pace's family in piercing cross-examination that made them seem heartless, vindictive, petty, and mean, and the sole origin of suspicion against the poor widow, as seen when the defense attorney questioned Harry Pace's mother:

Mr. Birkett.—Is it a fact that you, the mother, never rendered one moment's assistance in nursing the son?

Answer: No, she did not want me.

Q. Did you ever stay the night and nurse?

A. I don't remember.

Q. She had had a baby, and the baby was sick. That was enough for one woman, was it not?

A. Of course it was.

And so on through the conclusion of the prosecutor's case. By then it was apparent that there was no direct evidence that Beatrice Pace was the poisoner, and, beyond the finding of arsenic at autopsy, the victim's family really had nothing solid in terms of motive on which to rest its suspicion of Beatrice. If she had a lover at the time of her husband's death, he was not in evidence.

Given the public clamor both inside and outside the courtroom, the judge's next action made perfect sense. The judge concluded the proceedings with a speech. "In my opinion," he said, "it would not be safe to ask any jury to find a verdict of guilty on the evidence you have heard." The judge then directed the jurors to enter a verdict of not guilty, which they did. Beatrice Pace was free to go.

Her attorney turned to her and said, "And that's that, Mrs. Pace."

Robbed of the opportunity to present her full defense, destroy the reputation of her deceased husband (and father of her many children), and testify on her own behalf, Beatrice Pace managed to capitalize on the public appetite for her life story by selling it to a women's magazine for a small fortune. She bought a home in Gloucestershire and lived a long life in seclusion as Beatrice Martin, never speaking of the case for the public again. Judging by grainy old photos alone, she was one of those rare beauties who grew more attractive as age softened her features. She never remarried. She passed away in 1973 and took the truth to her grave.

GERTRUDE
GIBSON
PATTERSON

THE VICTIM: Charles A. Patterson

WHEN: May 5, 1911

WHERE: Denver, Colorado, near the E. B. Hendrie Mansion (now the Von Richthofen Castle)

DEFENSE COUNSEL: O. N. Hilton

THE CASE

A beautiful woman once aimed a gun at her husband as he knelt in the grass before her outside a tuberculosis clinic in the Rocky Mountains. He pleaded for his life. She shot him. He dropped to his hands and knees, begging her to stop, but she shot him again. Then she tucked the gun beneath his body and stumbled into a nearby house. An eyewitness followed her inside to find her slumped in a chair. The witness demanded to know the identity of the man she just killed. "He is my husband," she replied. "He wronged me." The authorities of Colorado did not appreciate the slaying one bit, and after much ado, Gertrude Patterson found herself facing a jury.[1]

On direct, Gertrude spoke of her late husband as a brute and a thug who began beating her shortly after their wedding and worse, forced her into intimacies with a wealthy man. At one time, she said, her husband "sold" her to a man named Strouss. She grew weary of compromising her morality for her husband, she said. "She appeared perfectly at ease," a reporter noted, "and told her story in a carefully modulated voice." The truth was even stranger than she had the power to explain.

When she was just sixteen, Gertrude Gibson met a wealthy Chicago industrialist, Emil Strouss, who kept her in luxury and pretended for her family's sake that they were married. Five years into their unwedded bliss, Gertrude found herself at a skating rink meeting a handsome young man to whom she was attracted, despite his terrible cough. She fell in love with Charles Patterson and worked up the courage to tell her old man about him. Thus formed the love triangle that featured her at its apex: "After his talk with Mr. Patterson, Mr. Strouss came to me and said that he was glad that the biggest thing in life had come to me and he wanted me to be happily married. It wasn't until some little time afterward that I learned that I had been made the dupe of two men. Imagine my feelings. I was crazed with sorrow." It seems the two men in her life had struck a bargain. Emil Strouss would share his fortune with Charles Patterson, and Charles Patterson would share his wife with Emil Strouss. All of this was quite interesting to the press, but it failed to fully explain why she shot her husband.

The prosecutor then subjected her to vigorous cross-examination that proved many discrepancies and mistruths in her testimony. Then he attacked her character with pointed questions. Wasn't it true that she was thrown out of school at an early age for immoral conduct? And wasn't it true that she once frequented a certain dive in St. Louis? Didn't she use the alias "Gertrude Knight"? Didn't she act as a proprietress for a resort in the seedy district of St. Louis? A pallor settled over her features as she weakly denied the barrage of accusations.

Later in jail, Gertrude objected to the cross-examination. "My God, don't take me back to that stand," she said. "That man Benson is murdering me by degrees and I can't stand it any longer. If he would only ask questions that were true I would not mind, but he has been asking questions that have no meaning and are lies. Someone has been telling him infamous lies about me, and he is killing me by inches. Why, I would rather die in the electric chair than go through what I have in the past week."

She would never find out. Her expensive attorney managed to find a witness who testified under oath that Gertrude's husband attacked her and knocked her down before he was shot. This witness later vanished, but the jury had heard enough. Gertrude was acquitted after six ballots. Crowds outside the courtroom cheered the result and bestowed kisses and best wishes on the freed killer.

Said the victim's mother, "If women can go and shoot down their husbands with no more provocation than Gertrude Patterson had, then I say it is up to the relatives of the victims of such women to deal summary justice. . . . Perhaps the same fate meted to her that she gave to my son would come closer to being the fair thing."

Said the victim's brother, himself an attorney, "The verdict means that a pretty woman can commit murder and get away with it. I know from my practice that conviction of a woman criminal is almost impossible."[2]

Gertrude herself was convinced the prosecutor was to blame for the outcome of her case. "Mr. Benson's vitriolic speech against me" helped her win the sympathy of the jury. "He made the mistake of dragging me deeper in the mire than I ever fell."

Her parting words for the public were, "From now on Gertrude Patterson will be a good woman." From all accounts, she was.

NAN PATTERSON

THE VICTIM: Francis Thomas Young, aka Frank Young, aka Caesar Young

WHERE: On West Broadway near Franklin Street, New York, New York

WHEN: June 4, 1904

DEFENSE COUNSEL: Abraham Levy

THE CASE

An enclosed, horse-drawn, two-seat cab was trotting down a busy city thoroughfare when the report of a pistol startled the horse. The shot came from inside the cab. As onlookers gathered, a policeman opened the door to see the body of a man slumped in the lap of a young woman. He had been shot in the chest.

She cried out, "Oh, Caesar! Caesar! What have you done?" a great many times. The cab made for the hospital, but Caesar Young was dead before they got there, and the young lady soon found herself in the Tombs suffering from a sudden onset of regular fainting spells.

The first examination Nan Patterson had to undergo was of her face and her full, womanly figure. The newspapers of New York found in her "no raving beauty," but there was no doubt the twenty-one-year-old capitalized on what she had. In the age of the Gibson Girl, whalebone corsets, and the hourglass figure, Nan modeled "the curved, buxom, high-pompadoured fashion that was the vogue in 1904."[1] The *Evening Telegram* parsed her appearance as "decidedly striking, and although she might not be termed beautiful she is a woman who would quickly

This portrait of Nan Patterson was widely circulated in the press. (From the George Grantham Bain Collection [Library of Congress].)

attract attention and would be termed good looking." The *New York Herald* was generous and clever, managing to bury the lede in its description of her, alluding in the final word to the magnificent chest that was then bewitching the press corps, describing her as "a woman of more than ordinary attraction. Her hair, which is dark brown, was massed on the top of her head yesterday under a becoming hat with just enough color in it to make it noticeable. Her eyes are blue and her features are regular. When she was arrested her fingers were covered with rings, most of them of great value. She had a heavy gold chain around her neck and a diamond pin in her bosom." Having gotten a good, long look at her, the New York press corps begged for more.

Nan Patterson was a spoiled Southern belle from Washington, DC, who was first married at sixteen to one Leon Martin, who found her beautiful and "strongly magnetic." (He would later blame himself for her troubles, for he was the one who moved her to New York and introduced her to "a fast crowd.") Drawn to the lights of Broadway, she left her husband in less than a year. Nan took her mother's maiden name of Randolph, as it conjured a possible connection to *the* Randolphs, American elites. She found some modest success (despite what everyone agreed was a dearth of any genuine talent) and had a chorus girl part in one of many traveling editions of the popular musical *Floradora*. Her moral code was an accommodating one, and we can further deduce her lifestyle and character from her choice of companion.

She met him on a train, and before long she was living in sin with Caesar Young, an English-born off-track bookie who, like Nan, had lax morals, expensive tastes, and a spouse somewhere. A business partner warned Caesar that Nan Patterson was trouble, a "mercenary, designing woman," but Caesar was infatuated with her. He made promises of securing a divorce; he financed her divorce from Mr. Martin. The sporting papers spread gossip about the notorious affair involving Caesar and the showgirl. Caesar's friends pressured him to end it.

At one point Caesar reconciled with his long-suffering wife. He continued to secretly send telegrams to his mistress, however, and at one point enjoyed a days-long rendezvous with her in Chicago's Hotel Wellington. But Nan knew her hold on her wealthy lover was slipping since he moved back in with his wife. She begged him to procure the promised divorce, but he again hesitated and begged patience. She grew disillusioned, sensing the end was near. Then her sister informed her that a friend of Caesar Young revealed that Caesar never had any intention of marrying Nan. On hearing this news, Nan went "absolutely wild," her sister said, capable of doing "something serious." The vacillating man then left his wife once again and moved into a hotel suite with his mistress, registering as "J. B. Patterson and Wife." Days later, he surprised her with a scheme to put her on a boat to London and thus to be rid of her for good. Not surprisingly, the love-struck Nan refused. "I don't want to go!" she said. "I don't feel that I can leave you. If you would go with me and we could jump off the boat together and die in each other's arms I would be very happy and willing to go."

Caesar did not heed her warning. He insisted on her move to England.

She declared she could not go because she was pregnant (which she wasn't).

He counseled her to end the pregnancy at once—in London. "They have just as good doctors in London as in New York."

Finally, she threw her arms around him and said, "Caesar, I love you more than Mrs. Young. Why don't you send her away and not send me?"

"Tut, tut, Nan. Chuck it," he said. "You know we must part."

She simply refused. Caesar and his wife then decided they would have to be the ones to leave town, so Mrs. Young made plans for a two-month "second honeymoon," booking passage on a luxury cruise to Europe aboard the *Germanic*.

Caesar told his mistress about the trip. In response, Nan acquired a pistol.

They quarreled in public on what would be their last night together. He slapped her across the face and left her in tears.

The next day, Caesar Young was in a cab, headed for the waterfront and a bon voyage, when that same pistol was fired into his chest, killing him almost instantly.

She was just a chorus girl who killed her married lover in a bad break-up, but on the witness stand and in the press, she was "a dewy rose." Admirers filled her jail cell with flowers and candy. In one day, she received two offers of marriage from midwestern farmers who had fallen in love with her picture, had a weakness for theatrical women, and were willing to give her "a respectable home," assuming she would soon quit her present home behind bars. But her focus as her trial loomed was on her wardrobe. "I looked over my dresses to see what I would wear for the trial," she told a reporter. "I finally picked one, but would you believe it, I couldn't get it on, I've got so fat. So I had to have a new one made, and my dressmaker was here this morning and will be here this afternoon to fit it. It's just a plain black gown with a white front to the waist. I don't want to wear anything flashy, but I am anxious to make a good appearance." She struck a fashion plate for the ages as she walked from the Tombs across the Bridge of Sighs and into the Supreme Court building on November 3, 1904, to stand trial on the romantic charge of first-degree premeditated murder in a full-skirted gown of black voile with veil, gloves, and a picture hat with a jaunty black ostrich plume.

She lifted the veil from her pale face to begin her testimony. She told the jury that her lover bade her farewell with these final words: "I have lost a lot of money and now I am going to lose my girl." The next thing she heard was a "muffled sound," and he fell. She insisted she never even saw the pistol. She swore she did not shoot him—he must have shot himself while she was looking the other way. Yet the evidence would show that the pistol was found in the pocket of the dead man's coat. On such a record, they should have had her dead to rights. Nothing about Caesar Young's conduct leading up to that moment or his purported final words supported a theory of suicide. Her version of the story made no psychological sense. She should have gone straight from the Tombs to the chair. But she had Abraham Levy.

Nan Patterson had retained the most famous criminal trial lawyer in New York in that day, an advocate whom famous true crime reporter Alexander Woollcott dubbed "the mighty Abe Levy . . . the most adroit and zestful practitioner of the criminal law in this country." He was a lawyer's lawyer, the equivalent of an English barrister. All of his clients were referred to him by other attorneys. Over the course of his career, he appeared in more than three hundred homicide cases. Whenever he was in trial, the courtroom was packed with acolytes and admirers, including young playwright Bayard Veillier, who found his best ideas by following Abe Levy from court to court. As Levy's son would recall of Levy, "One of his outstanding professional attributes was a suavity of manner and unfailing courtesy to the court. Many judges have told me that he was the most gracious lawyer who ever appeared before them, but beneath his courteous manner was the dynamic force of a powerful personality. He was a mighty cross-examiner." In this instance, however, it was his power to direct the exam of his client that would decide the case.

"Nan, look at me," her attorney said. "Did you shoot Caesar Young?"

"I did not," she said calmly. "I swear I did not. God knows if I could bring him back to life I would!"

The true test came when the prosecutor quizzed her for more than two hours. She kept her composure and her answers brief.

Prosecutor Wm. Rand: Were you feeling in good spirits on the night of June third?

Defendant: Yes.

Q. You loved him passionately, devoutly; he was the one man in the world for you?

A. Yes.

Q. And he was going away on the morrow with his wife?

A. Yes.

Q. And still you were happy, knowing that he was going away?

A. I knew he was going away, but I did not think he would be away long. . . .

But it didn't matter whether the state's attorney's arrows found their mark. The papers declared the defendant victorious, brave in the face of the grinding machine of the merciless state. Her attorney held a Christian Gospel and gave an impassioned "cast the first stone" speech. When he concluded, "from the rear of the courtroom sobs could be heard from the audience."

Though it was a tough act to follow, Prosecutor Rand's subsequent effort compelled many to the inescapable conclusion that Nan Patterson committed murder. The prosecutor's summing-up had the courtroom holding its breath for three hours as he tore apart Nan's flimsy testimony. Even the defense attorney yielded the palm to his opposing counsel. "In all my 24 years' experience at the New York bar," Abe Levy declared, "I have never heard such a speech. It was a marvel of advocacy."

The jury deliberated until it could not deliberate anymore and declared itself hung at six to six. Thus, the whole damn thing had to be done all over again. A second trial brought about the same result. The state tried a third time to convict Nan Patterson of murder one. This time, they had the case reassigned to a judge known as "The Terror," Recorder John W. Goff. Universally described as Satan in a black robe, he was cruel and sadistic, and was thus perhaps willing to send a woman to the electric chair.

This time, the emphasis was on the medical evidence as physician after physician described the autopsy of the victim, the location of the wounds, and the unlikelihood that they were self-inflicted. In rebuttal, Abe Levy pointed out that the original coroner's report had listed the cause of Caesar Young's death as suicide. He hung onto that point throughout the trial, and he knew how to draw out a moment. "When Levy made a point," an observer remarked, "and he had made a good one here, he hung on to it with grim tenacity. It will be observed that he was not only cross-examining, he was summing up all the time. When he finished with this part of the examination it was indelibly impressed on the minds of the jurors that this witness, this veteran of thousands of autopsies, had concluded from what he had seen that Caesar Young had committed suicide."

It was all over except for the crying. A throng of thousands awaited the third verdict, and for a third time the jury was hung. The final count was eight in favor of convicting her of manslaughter, and four held out for acquittal. The state finally admitted that further proceedings would be unavailing, and Nan Patterson was released. She walked out of her attorney's office one last time and took up a singing career. News of her liberation had spread to vaudeville, where she took to the stage "pompadoured and buxom, clad in an attractive pink dress. . . . She was terrible."

When her career failed her, she got married, then married again until she found a man who could keep her in luxury. She lived out a comfortable life in Seattle, far away from the lights of Broadway and the opinions of jurors.

ALMA RATTENBURY

THE VICTIM: Francis Mawson Rattenbury
WHEN: March 28, 1935
WHERE: Bournemouth, England
DEFENSE COUNSEL: T. J. O'Connor, KC

THE CASE

On a Sunday evening in the spring of 1935, a well-known sixty-seven-year-old architect was sleeping in a chair in his drawing room when he was struck on the head three times with a blunt object, suffering wounds from which he would not recover. When the police arrived and quizzed the household, they noticed that the dying man's thirty-eight-year-old wife was very drunk—and she was confessing to the crime. She was so intoxicated that she forgot herself entirely and tried to kiss some of the police officers assembled in her house. Alma Rattenbury told the police in no uncertain terms that she killed her husband, Francis Rattenbury. "That is right—I did it deliberately, and would do it again." The authorities took her for her word and charged her with murder.

Just about everyone in England and beyond formed the opinion that it was an open-and-shut case, which made the trial that followed all the more spectacular for the surprises that lay in store when the whole truth won out. But first, Mrs. Rattenbury's moral failings (and there were many) would come to light.

Mrs. Rattenbury had been Alma Victoria Clark, a Canadian by birth who was "very attractive to men," as one scholar of the case has remarked.

"In the witness box she still showed as a very elegant woman. She was well and quietly dressed in dark blue. She had a pale face, with a beautiful egg-like line of the jaw, dark grey eyes, and a mouth with a very full lower lip."[1] Observers learned along with the court that Alma Rattenbury had a complicated love life. She had been married three times, first to a serviceman who was killed in action in the war; then she began seeing a married man, who eventually left his wife for Alma. The marriage failed and they separated. Alma then met a married architect who was sixty years old to her thirty-one. Francis Rattenbury eventually became Alma's third husband. So great was the scandal where they resided, the May-December lovers decided to move to a new community and begin a new life together in Bournemouth, England.

The Rattenbury marriage appeared to have been one of mere convenience, and soon enough the young bride of the elder architect would have cause to lament her choice in husband. Alma has been called "a natural born bad picker" of men. Moreover, she had poor taste. The evidence would soon reveal that Alma had been having a love affair with a servant young enough to be her son. Another person came forward to claim the crime as his own because he could not bear to see Alma punished for the crime: the Rattenburys' eighteen-year-old chauffeur, George Percy Stoner, a young man described by the police as "reserved and introspective."

A love triangle had taken on its ancient shape. Both Mrs. Rattenbury and her teenage lover each tried to take all the blame for the murder, revealing a mutual willingness to sacrifice the self for the other. Alma and George were charged with murder together, and "the Rattenbury-Stoner case" earned its eternal moniker. Each faced the death penalty, but still they did not turn on one another. George Stoner refused to testify; he chose not to fight his case. As true crime author F. Tennyson Jesse observed, "One of the most interesting points in this case is, that is the only one, as far as I am aware, where two people have been charged together on the capital indictment when neither of the accused has abandoned the other in a scramble for safety."

The evidence revealed moral failings on the part of every member of the triangle that had formed the previous September, when the Rattenburys advertised for a chauffeur. Young George Stoner replied to the advertisement and took the job; within days he and the lady of the house were lovers. Clearly it appeared that she worshipped her young lover, perhaps undeservedly so for he had little beyond charming blond looks and virility to recommend him as a man. "Mrs. Rattenbury was a highly sexed woman," explained one of her biographers, "and six years of being deprived of sexual satisfaction had combined with the tuberculosis from which she suffered, to bring her to the verge of nymphomania."

In the meantime, Mr. Rattenbury had apparently decided to look aside at this. During the trial, Mr. Justice Humphreys referred to Francis Rattenbury as being "that very unpleasant character for which, I think, we have no suitable expression, but which the French call 'a mari complaisant.' A man who knew that his wife was committing adultery, and had no objection to it." He did indeed seem completely incurious when his wife fell in love with a teenager. And yet fall in love they did, as the details would vividly provide. It was counted strongly against their characters when she divulged on cross-examination that she had "connexion" (in the official language of the case) with her chauffeur-lover while her young son lay sleeping in the same room. Alma Rattenbury decided at the eleventh hour that she was going to tell the whole truth, regardless of the consequences. She told the jury with a shame-filled face that the truth was her lover had committed the attack on her husband and had told her of it only after the fact.

It would only seem obvious to her in hindsight, but by seducing this much younger man, Mrs. Rattenbury had unleashed in him emotions beyond her ability to control. Had she stopped to think, she might have realized that a man of George's age and class would be overwhelmed by a "connexion" to her, and it may not be good for him in the grander scheme to become the sexual plaything of a much older woman who was also his social superior. Mr. Justice Humphreys shook a proverbial finger at her during the trial when he said, "She was committing adultery with her husband's servant in her bedroom, and in that bedroom in a little bed, there was a child of six. She spent money on this man in a different station from herself, buying him such things as silk pyjamas at three guineas."

Yet with these facts, her attorney was able to move the jurors to pity her. In his closing remarks in the defense of Alma Rattenbury, her attorney said, "I am not here to condone, still less to commend, her conduct. I am not here to cast one stone against that wretched boy whose position there in the dock may be due to folly and self-indulgence on her part, to which he fell a victim. I will say no more about what is past in Mrs. Rattenbury's life. I would only say that if you may be tempted to feel that she has sinned, that her sin has been great and has involved others who would never otherwise have been involved, that you should ask yourselves whether you or anybody of you are prepared first to cast a stone."

Her attorney went on in her defense. "You may as moral men and women, as citizens, condemn her in your souls for the part she has played. . . . She will bear to her grave the brand of reprobation, and men and women will know how she has acted. That will be her sorrow and her disgrace so long as she lives. You may think of Mrs. Rattenbury as a woman, self-indulgent and willful, who by her own acts and folly had erected in this poor young man a Frankenstein of jealousy which she could not control."

The speech saved Alma Rattenbury. She was found not guilty by the jury. Her lover did not fare as well. He was pronounced guilty, though the jury recommended mercy. Regardless, the penalty was mandatory. George Stoner was sentenced to death.

Four days passed. Alma had been acquitted by a jury and restored to her life, but she did not want it. Overcome by grief for her condemned lover, Alma bought a knife and took a train to a riverbank where once she had made love to George Stoner. She thrust the knife into her broken heart six times until she was dead.

The wave of sympathy that resulted probably saved the life of her lover. George Stoner was reprieved after 300,000 people signed a petition. He served seven years of his sentence before he was freed. He remained for the rest of his life condemned for the loss of one life and held indirectly responsible for the loss of another.

DAISY ROOT

THE VICTIM: Brenton "Brit" Root
WHEN: November 3, 1935
WHERE: Memphis, Tennessee
DEFENSE COUNSEL: A. B. Galloway

THE CASE

It was close to two o'clock in the morning when Daisy Root woke Brit Root. "Look at me, darling," she said. Then she shot him—four times in the torso and once in the wrist. Then she calmly picked up a phone and informed an astonished operator that she had just shot her husband.

The ambulance attendants could not save him. He was dead before he got to the hospital. Some would say—still say to this day—that Daisy Root did her kind a favor and rid Memphis of a scoundrel. Others blanch at his violent end, but none can look away from a beautiful woman in a peck of trouble for what the papers called A FLIRTATION SLAYING.[1]

Daisy Alexander Root, twenty-nine, was arrested at once for her husband's killing, but from the beginning the law was light on her. She was released to attend his funeral, where she wept copiously and garnered the immediate forgiveness and full support of her father-in-law, an Episcopal minister.

In contrast to the opinions of friends and family, the district attorney took a dim view of the matter, and Daisy Root found herself on the witness stand facing first-degree murder charges and a potential sentence of life in prison. Daisy told the story of her marriage and her troubles

Daisy Root on trial. (Special Collections, University of Memphis Libraries.)

with her husband, who was not only promiscuous but conscientious about it; he kept a list of his conquests and photo albums of his affairs. She told the story of the events leading up to the fatal shooting. The night before, Daisy and Brit had gone out together with friends to celebrate a lull in their marital wars. Heedless, Brit was paying close attention to a nineteen-year-old redheaded cigarette girl named Lucille, calling her sweet names. Daisy grew jealous and slapped him across the face, twice. He replied to this by declaring, "You can keep me from buying a pack of cigarettes from her, but you can't keep me from loving her." Daisy sobbed as she told the jury that she took her gun to her estranged husband's house because she "needed it for protection" in the countryside and she shot her husband because "he reached for his gun."

She underwent a vigorous cross-examination by the prosecutor. He proved that her marriage to Mr. Root had been "necessary" as she was pregnant with their son. He brought out the fact that Daisy herself had had an affair with the couple's realtor. The two got in a shouting match at one point. As bitterly as she fought with her husband over his womanizing, she fought with the prosecutor. It was put to her that she killed her husband because he flirted with other girls and made her mad. She never really loved the man; she was a hell-raiser.

"It's a lie—oh, you know it's a lie!" she "almost screamed," the reporters said, as the state's attorney shouted at her, "Don't you know that you never loved Brenton Root?"

It was effective. The jury convicted Daisy Root of second-degree murder. She was sentenced to ten years in prison. Even so, she was allowed to be free on bail as she awaited the outcome of an appeal of her looming stretch.

The Supreme Court denied her appeal of the sentence. Daisy Root would get no relief from the appellate courts. In its opinion, however, the court went on to bemoan the "many indignities" the defendant suffered at her victim's hands. The court suggested that the governor of the state take up the case and consider commuting her sentence. The court noted the extenuating circumstances, commenting that the trial testimony revealed that Brit Root's conduct before his slaying was "lecherous in the extreme," as he "seems to have maintained illicit relations with literally scores of women." Governor Browning soon acted, issuing an order reducing both charge and sentence, meaning Daisy Root was as free as air.

The *New York Times* was among the newspapers who met this twist in the tale with howls of derision in banner headlines. CUTS RAGE SLAYER'S TERM was its outraged summary of the governor's action.

Daisy Root went on to marry again and live out the quiet life of a pardoned woman in Tennessee.

ABE SADA

THE VICTIM: Ishida Kichizô
WHEN: May 1936
WHERE: Japan
DEFENSE COUNSEL: Takeuchi Kintarô

THE CASE

After spending days making love to him, Abe Sada strangled her lover, carved her name in his flesh, pocketed his genitals, and vanished. The most panicked headlines to ever appear above a woman's name were seen throughout Japan:

GROTESQUE MURDER IN OGU RED-LIGHT DISTRICT

BLOOD CHARACTERS CARVED IN MASTER'S CORPSE

BEAUTIFUL MAID DISAPPEARS FOLLOWING LOVE TRYST

Stirred to the hunt, Japanese police captured her four long days later in Tokyo. One would think that an appropriate punishment would await Jill the Ripper, this actual living example of the fabled female *lustmörder innen*[1]—but Abe Sada, thirty-two, was an ENCHANTINGLY BEAUTIFUL FLOWER OF EVIL. Additionally, she appeared to be lucid, and she offered the stunned world a levelheaded explanation for her repugnant acts: She did it all "because I loved him."[2]

A pretty child from a poor family, Abe Sada grew up to become a geisha, then a prostitute. She worked at low-end brothels, was occasionally questioned by police for theft, earned a reputation for throwing tantrums, and contracted syphilis. She lived this TALE OF HORROR FROM THE HELL OF LUSTFUL DESIRE until she was rescued by a married, middle-class restaurant owner. She would tell the police that Ishida Kichizô was her first true love. The two of them would spend all the time they could in bed together, gorging themselves on sex for days, going without food, not even stopping to bathe, as described in detailed newspaper accounts of the lovers' final days together.

Abe Sada later proclaimed she was madly in love with the man she strangled. She wanted him—forever. She knew he was not the type who would leave his wife and run off with his mistress. She had suggested they commit suicide together, but he shrugged off this remark. The idea then came to her to take his life. "I looked at this man's sleeping face," she later confessed, "and thought that since I was in no position to become his wife, no matter how much I loved him, in the end he would belong to another woman, which would be a pity. I thought it would be better to kill him."

She pawned some clothes and bought a knife and began threatening Ishida with it. He did not take her seriously. "When I put the edge against the base of his penis," Abe would later confess, "and said that I would make sure he wouldn't fool around with other women, he just laughed and said that I was being stupid."

The Japanese press knew that this mutilation was a WEIRD INCIDENT BARELY SEEN IN THE HISTORY OF CRIME. Penis-severing is thankfully almost unheard of. In the United States, Lorena Bobbitt is remembered for merely trying to dismember her husband as revenge for his unhusband-like conduct (it was found and reattached).[3]

In Abe Sada's case, it was not revenge, she insisted; it was love that motivated her, and she "cut off the part of the man I loved the most." Questioned for days, she continually spoke of their love for one another. "He is underground, happy that I killed him. I feel good, as though something has been completed."

When Abe Sada went on trial for her life in November 1936, the courthouse was overrun with young women in the throes of Sada mania who gasped at the exhibit of genitals in a jar and were barred from hearing her actual confession and plea of guilty to the charges. In the sentencing phase of the proceedings, Abe faced the possibility of death at the hands of a three-judge panel. Her sentence was fixed: six years.

Photos of Abe Sada taken shortly after her arrest appeared in the press for decades. (From the *Madison [Wisconsin] State Journal,* March 14, 1976, via News paperarchive.com.)

The lead judge later explained his reasoning for such a light punishment in a blunt official statement on the case (just as he would one day point-blank admit that he frequented harlots and that her case had aroused him). Abe Sada's act was simply "one of love taken to an extreme," the judge said, and besides, the dead man was to blame: "The victim in this crime was himself lascivious and old enough to understand the consequences of his actions. Without consideration for his family or household, he engaged in sexual excess for over ten days with the defendant, making himself the subject of sexual indulgences, a play-thing for the defendant's whims. Without restraint he fulfilled her desires. In this way, it is impossible to overlook how he was central in causing this crime."

Abe Sada went to prison for a time, but the emperor of Japan granted her a pardon, shortening her time served to five years. She went into semiseclusion, hounded by the press and a public still eager for details. "Abe Sada sold print," as historian William Johnston explained, "because her name conjured up lurid images that mixed the erotic and the violent. It signified an imagined figure, that of the sexually dangerous woman in a man's world." Her infamy has now spanned generations and spurred authors and filmmakers to retell the story of the woman who was so bad she's good.

MADELINE SMITH

> Let a female delinquent be young and we can overlook her
> degenerate type, and even regard her as beautiful; the sexual
> instinct misleading us here as it does in making us attribute
> to women more of sensitiveness and passion than they really
> possess. And in the same way, when she is being tried on a
> criminal charge, we are inclined to excuse, as noble impulses of
> passion, acts which arise from the most cynical calculations.
> > —Dr. Cesare Lombroso and William Ferrero, *The*
> > *Female Offender*

THE VICTIM: Emile L'Angelier
WHEN: March 23, 1857
WHERE: Glasgow, Scotland
DEFENSE COUNSEL: John Inglis (afterward Lord Glencorse)

THE CASE

Every collector of the stories of the femme fatale will eventually come across a lady who proves mesmeric. William Roughead (the prolific Scotsman who holds the crown as Europe's finest true crime author) may have been the most well-read man on the subject who ever lived. Of all the female killers he studied, he had five "darker favorites," including Jessie McLachlan,[1] Florence Bravo,[2] Florence Maybrick,[3] and Adelaide Bartlett. Each woman was young, attractive, accused of murder, and by many accounts (including Roughead's), morally insane.

In his later years, the murder fancier stumbled on the dusty tale of a homicide involving a woman of superior social standing who was, to him, "figuratively speaking—virgin," and he was enraptured. She was Madeline Smith, Glasgow socialite. Her father was a prominent architect who owned a house in town, owned a house in the country, and had six servants to spoil his children.[4] One day the eldest daughter of fortune was walking the streets when she met the eyes of a young Frenchman, Emile L'Angelier. They became lovers, and Madeline Smith penned erotic letters to him that left no doubt ("Beloved, if we did wrong last night it was in the excitement of our love").[5] Then she found a man of superior rank who was interested in her, and she tried to extract herself from her first relationship—to no avail. Her French lover gave her grief. Madeline then applied a witch's solution to the universal problem of shaking a lover who won't let go. She gave him chocolates laced with arsenic.

To author Roughead, Madeline Smith was "matchless," his "heroine." He resurrected her case and reintroduced her to a world thirsty for bloody muses.[6] The same murderess equally enthralled another illustrious author, American novelist Henry James. Like Roughead, James searched for years for a portrait of Madeline Smith. She forever eluded them both. They, and we, must settle for a vague newspaper sketch of the heroine on trial.

Madeline Smith had to face her accusers alone, as her parents declined to attend their daughter's murder trial. During the criminal proceedings, all of her correspondence was read aloud as she proudly kept her chin up, intriguing the masses with her nonchalance. Her attorney, John Inglis, gave a speech that is still famous in the annals of the bar of Scotland. In it, he denounced the murder victim as an adventurer and seducer who was trying to ruin a young girl's life.[7]

The jury was out half an hour before it declared the case "not proven." Madeline vanished into obscurity, leaving behind that one profile sketch of her looking proud and defiant, along with her love letters—the poetry of a poisoner.

As to her attorney, John Inglis would become noted for just one remark that he made in connection with Miss Madeline Smith: "I would sooner have danced than supped with her."

MARGUERITE
STEINHEIL

THE VICTIMS: Adolphe Steinheil and Madame Japy
WHEN: May 31, 1908
WHERE: Paris, France
DEFENSE COUNSEL: Antony Aubin

THE CASE

On February 16, 1899, Felix Faure, the president of the Republic of France, slipped away from his official duties for a rendezvous with his mistress Marguerite, better known as Mme Steinheil, wife of lesser-known artist Adolphe Steinheil and a celebrated beauty in Paris.

Perhaps they were merely conversing in one another's arms at the fateful moment, though popular legend has it that Mme Steinheil was situated in what might today be alluded to as a Lewinsky *grande plié* when the excitement became too great for President Faure's heart to bear; the organ ceased. It was said that he died with his hand entangled in her hair, which had to be cut away to free her.[1] Mme Steinheil became even more widely celebrated for her charms—or rather, their effect.

But it was another circumstance altogether when, a few years later, another man turned up dead in her home—the cuckold, M. Steinheil, her husband—as his corpse was accompanied by the body of Mme Japy, Marguerite Steinheil's stepmother.

It was a bizarre scene indeed in the bedchamber of Mme Steinheil on the morning of May 31, 1908. Her husband lay strangled to death, her stepmother also murdered, and the famous enchantress herself was bound and gagged but curiously uninjured. When freed from her bonds, she told of a burglary committed the evening before: four people—three men dressed in robes and a woman with red hair—had attacked the household, robbed them of jewelry and money, killed her husband and stepmother, and left them all as they were found.

Or at least that was the sole survivor's version of events. The Paris police soon developed a more plausible theory: Mme Steinheil herself admitted an assassin to kill her spouse, and Mme Japy, attracted to the commotion, by necessity became a second victim. So convinced were the detectives that they sought to persuade a jury of her guilt, and she was put on trial in the Paris Assize Court to determine whether she ought to stretch her neck beneath the guillotine.

From the very beginning, the prosecutors looked to Mme Steinheil's stunning past for evidence of a sinful intent. She was born in Beaucourt, in a Germanic region of France, in 1869. Her father was from a very wealthy family, and her mother was the unusually beautiful daughter of a local innkeeper. Marguerite grew into a very privileged and indulged young lady. She made her debut at seventeen and promptly fell in love with a lieutenant, but her hypocritical father refused to bless the love match. She was heartbroken.

When she was twenty, her family took her to meet a better marriage prospect, an old painter named Steinheil. She detested him on sight, calling him "a shortish man of at least forty, thin, with small eyes, a dark moustache, and a pointed beard." "No thank you!" she cried. "I'd never dream of marrying a man like that. Why, I'd look as though I were his daughter!"

But Steinheil was deeply in love. He shaved the objectionable graying beard. He invited her to watch him paint cathedral frescoes. He told her about his grand home on the Impasse Ronsin in Paris. She became gradually interested, and one passionless proposal later, they were married in 1890. A monthlong Italian honeymoon was to follow, but ten days into the adventure, she was so depressed that she begged him to take her back to her mother. He did, but he persuaded her to at least come to Paris to see her fabulous new home. Her family nudged her to Paris, and she entered the much-fabled house she'd still not seen. Though it was grand, newlywed Mme Steinheil found fault; at the sight of all the dust and the smell of fried onions, she burst into tears.

Adolphe Steinheil did what he could to soothe his young bride, and he cajoled her into posing for his miniatures in oil. She came to believe "he liked me chiefly because I am small." After the first few weeks of misery, she realized that her husband was "indifferent, easily satisfied, and compared life to a disagreeable pill which everyone must swallow . . . our married life was doomed and happiness impossible." She determined to divorce him, but after some long conversations, the Steinheils agreed to remain married but to be "friends" and to live with "full liberty." Remarked she, "No one ever guessed that, although living under one roof, my husband and I were separated. Indeed, this way had many advantages, and even the most united couples should adopt it."

Marguerite found new passions. Many new passions. She opened her salon and her heart, and one of the first to enter was the sculptor Bartholdi, creator of "Liberty Illuminating the World" (the Statue of Liberty, New York harbor). He was everything her husband was not: a gifted artist who applied himself on a grand scale and a monumentally egotistical man. On one occasion he told her, "The Americans believe that it is Liberty that illumines the world, but, in reality, it is my genius."

And there were other men. One was the romantic, sensuous attorney general, M. B., who called almost every day. Another was M. H., the distinguished author. Then there was the Comte de B.; M. X., the minister of state; M. T., the famous banker who enjoyed bacchanalian orgies in a secret room of his country estate; the painter Bonnat; the composer Massenet; the poet Coppee; and diplomats, artists, generals, scientists, and judges—"a whole body of judges." And of course the president.

So when her husband and mother turned up dead, the prosecutors at the Assize Court put her on trial as much for her wicked ways as for double murder. Needless to say, the newspapermen went rabid and infected the public with feverish speculations. Was there a political motive in the killings? Was the true object of the robbery a set of compromising letters in her possession?

The case set Paris crazy with excitement, and it seems that a majority of men favored acquittal, while the ladies almost universally believed her guilty. Some newspapers lamented the fact that French juries are not sequestered, which would allow the panel to return home at night "where they are subjected to the possible influence of their wives." The courtroom filled to overcrowding and was frequently in an uproar as the state presented its case.

Everything she'd ever done was brought forth for public inspection, every fault amplified into a felony. The prosecutor called a governess who testified that as a child of five, Marguerite often lied. The prosecutor thought much of this. He also called as a witness her first lover, Lieutenant Sheffer, to testify to their little romance and further establish her amorality at a young age. They set about proving that no money and no jewels were taken from the home as she claimed. They tried to prove that she attempted to finger her servants for the murders.

The prosecution's chief witness was Mme Steinheil's latest lover, a rich merchant named Borderel. But this witness backfired on them by undermining the theory that she slayed her husband to marry Borderel. Marriage was not contemplated between us, Borderel said, concluding his testimony by saying that he didn't think her guilty.

Mme Steinheil then took the stand herself, and she was grilled mercilessly. "You are a great actress," remarked the prosecutor. "You play your part well."

"Alas, it is not acting," she retorted. "I am but a poor woman fighting for her life.

"When a poor weak woman has been for seven hours a day for many days under the badgering of a magistrate, who never ceases to repeat, 'I know you are guilty, you killed your husband and your mother,' when your mind is tortured, your spirit broken, contradictions are not unnatural."

Then another young man, an "unknown in Paris," took the stand and admitted that he participated in the burglary-murders while dressed as a red-haired woman. The defendant fainted. The prosecutors denounced him as insane, but the damage to their case was done. The jury deliberated for two and a half hours and announced its acquittal to thunderous cheers. It was reported that a crowd of tens of thousands stood outside the courthouse to celebrate the result.

Mme Steinheil fled the scene in a motorcar and soon quitted France altogether, choosing London for a new life. In June 1917, she married a baron and became Lady Abinger. In crude early film footage of her wedding, she wears a white gown and radiant smile. She died in 1954 and perhaps faced a higher tribunal than the city of Paris could ever muster.

‡ ‡ ‡

For more information: Marguerite Steinheil, *My Memoirs* (London: E. Nash, 1912).

The Red Widow Mystery

Two Unsolved Murders That Shed Unexpected Light on the Strange Death of a President of France

By THEODORE ROSCOE

CONSIDER, as a Frenchman might say, the extreme frightfulness which shocked Paris during the night of May 30, 1908, in the studio of Adolphe Steinheil, popular portrait painter and nephew of the great Meissonier, on the Impasse Ronsin.

Remy Couillard, M. Steinheil's valet, found the artist in the bathroom, strangled. In the next room lay his mother-in-law, Madame Japy, garroted.

In a near-by bedroom was the artist's beautiful wife, Marguerite, bound hand and foot, a gag tied tightly between her teeth.

To Chief Inspector Octave Hamard of the Bureau Surete, Marguerite Steinheil related an astounding story.

"The clock was striking midnight," she told him, "when I was awakened by a hand over my mouth. Three black-bearded men and a woman were around my bed. They wore long black cloaks and queer, conical hats.

"One of the men said:

"'Give us the jewels and the papers or we will kill you, your husband and your mother.'

"I fainted and when I came to, hours later, I did not know what had happened until Remy found me."

Remy had heard nothing. Neither had the cook, nor her son. No one in the neighborhood had seen weird, cloaked figures.

Whoever they were, they had rummaged through Marguerite's bureau, ransacked a desk, and, she said, stolen pearls worth $100,000.

Were the pearls registered? No, they were the gift of a "friend."

And the papers? They were documents of a private nature.

The officers found no rope burns on her wrists or ankles, no mark of violence from the gag. The boulevards rocked with the sensation.

Then something must have shut Hamard's mouth. Politics? The inquest returned a verdict of: "Crime of debauchery; killers unknown."

Madame Steinheil left Paris.

Then five months after the murder, she telephoned a newspaper.

"I have just learned of a clue," Widow Steinheil declared. "The night before the tragedy, a costume shop on the Left Bank rented three black robes and false beards."

The costume shop proprietor recalled the incident clearly.

But Chief Inspector Hamard scented trickery. He sent Marguerite a photograph of a bearded American named Burlington. Marguerite identified the man as one of the assassins. Burlington furnished an alibi.

On November 10th she told a reporter she believed Remy Couillard guilty and suggested they search the valet's room.

In a floor crack under the valet's bed they found a pearl!

Then Marguerite Steinheil confessed that she had planted the pearl to scare Remy into a confession.

"Mariette, the cook, and her son Alexander are the murderers!" she sobbed to the confused police.

Mariette and Alexander hurled oaths at Marguerite, denouncing her and proved an alibi.

"Ask her why she sent the dog, Ture, away that night!" Mariette screamed. "Ask her why she sent her little daughter, Marthe, away. Ask her about her country villa! Ask her about her mysterious Aunt Lili!"

Hamard did ask, and learned that her villa had been the gift of a rich M. Borderel. Other men had provided gowns, jewels, a landaulet. To cover these tokens of friendship, Marguerite had invented a mythical "Aunt Lili."

When this news spread, the boulevards began to call Marguerite the "Red Widow."

She could not explain her daughter's absence nor why she sent away the watchdog.

On November 26th she was accused of the double murder.

Her lawyers stalled the trial for a year, and during this time a strange story was whispered.

This tale went back nine years to a night in February, 1899. On that evening (two nights after St.

The Steinheil Villa on the Impasse Ronsin, Scene of the Murders Which Rocked Paris.

Mme. Marguerite Steinheil, "Red Widow," and Close Friend of President Faure.

Valentine's Day) Mme. Steinheil went out. In an hour, she returned, in hysterics, her gown torn, her pompadour a tangled mass, and from one side tresses had been shorn away!

Steinheil ran to his wife's room.

"Marguerite—" he cried. Then he backed from the room without a word.

The maid never forgot the episode. The date was the same night the nation went into mourning for the sudden death of Felix Faure, President of France.

The "Red Widow" had been a frequent visitor at the Presidential Palace.

Crowds stormed the courtroom, offering as high as $250 for seats, when Marguerite's trial opened November 3rd, 1909.

Marguerite's letters, love life and laundry were held up to

The Second Floor of the Steinheil Villa, Where the "Red Widow's" Artist Husband and Mother Were Killed to Furnish One of France's Most Spectacular Mysteries.

the rage, laughter and tears of the crowd.

They applauded when Antony Aubin, for the defense, asked how a weak woman could strangle two people—"And why would she want to kill her mother?"

They wildly cheered the verdict of "Not guilty!"

Marguerite went into seclusion, a year later to publish her "Memoirs."

After her daughter was born, she wrote, she needed a holiday in the Alps, and at Thermignon she met Felix Faure.

Back in Paris, the President asked her at her home.

Faure made her his confidante, she wrote, and asked her to keep his secret documents. And finally, on St. Valentine's Day, 1899, he gave her the $100,000 string of pearls. Two nights later he was dead.

And it was these pearls, these papers, that the cloaked assassins were after nine years later.

Shortly after the World War broke out, she married an impoverished British peer, and faded from the picture.

In 1937, appeared a book—"The Story of Secret Service"—containing a curious echo to the "Red Widow" case.

The statement is made concerning Mata Hari, caught by the French in 1916: "She was removed to the prison of Saint Lazare and assigned to a cell which formerly had been occupied by Mme. Steinheil, whose pistol extinguished a President of the Republic."

A footnote to that revealing chapter gives the President's name as "Felix Faure."

The "Red Widow Mystery" as revisited by the *American Weekly* and published by the *San Antonio (Texas) Light,* January 30, 1944. (Via Newspaperarchive.com.)

VERA STRETZ

Where there's a beautiful woman in the dock, it makes a Court
trial so much more amusing!
> —Augustus Muir, *The Bronze Door*

THE VICTIM: Dr. Fritz Gebhardt
WHEN: November 25, 1935
WHERE: Beekman Tower, New York, New York
DEFENSE COUNSEL: Samuel S. Leibowitz

THE CASE

Stripped to its essentials, the death of Dr. Fritz Gebhardt certainly looked like a premeditated murder. The naked truth was that his mistress shot him and then parked herself on the steps leading to his apartment for a good cry.

Two patrolmen responding to "shots fired" calls found thirty-one-year-old Vera Stretz on the staircase. When an officer asked her what she had in her purse, which she was clutching at her side, she raised her tearstained face and replied, "Lipstick and my keys and a passport and my engagement ring, a compact and a handkerchief." The patrolman took it from her only to discover she also carried a .32 revolver that was warm to the patrolman's palm; a box of ammunition; two discharged shells; a passport in the name of Dr. Fritz Gebhardt, age forty-two, German financier; seven shares of B & O stock made out to Fritz Gebhardt; and a silk nightie with fresh bloodstains on it. It was mere moments into the investigation and she had already proved herself a liar and a thief. These are not recommended strategies for a would-be femme fatale.

Sharp, William. 1936. *The Vera Stretz Murder Trial*. (Albright-Knox Art Gallery, Buffalo, New York, USA. P2000:1.85 Gift of Frederic P. Norton, 2000. Photo credit: Albright-Knox Art Gallery / Art Resource, NY.)

However, he was about to be dubbed "the most attractive girl ever to be charged with first-degree murder in the state of New York."[1]

The patrolman asked the pretty lady if she happened to shoot anyone with her handgun.

"Yes, I did," cried the beautiful blond. "But please don't ask me why I did it." Apparently, she hadn't had time to get her story straight. But the State of New York would certainly soon insist that she explain herself in a proceeding known as *The People vs. Vera Stretz*.

Eventually Vera revealed to the police that she was a graduate of New York University, where she studied German. She taught for a while, but she stopped working when she received an inheritance of $35,000 from her mother. Vera met Dr. Fritz Gebhardt when both took a cruise on the SS *Vulcania* in December 1934. A whirlwind courtship followed. Vera moved into his apartment building, taking a place one floor below his. She took a part-time job with his import firm. He gave her a platinum engagement ring with a large diamond. Then she killed him. He died on the floor next to his bed, his feet entangled in a blood-spattered sheet. The medical examiner would later opine that some of his wounds may have been made by a woman's fingernails.

"Now, Miss Stretz, why did you kill this man?" asked Inspector Kear.

Vera did not follow the femme fatale protocol. She did not weep, faint, or tell a tale of woe. She would keep everyone who read a newspaper guessing as to her motive. To the police she simply said, "Please don't ask me that. I think I should talk to a lawyer first." Her father agreed to retain the best criminal lawyer then practicing in New York, Samuel Leibowitz, the scourge of every prosecutor in the city. He was famous because he had successfully defended a murder case, saving a client from the electric chair, 115 times in a row. Vera's case would either break his winning streak or make it 116 times in a row.[2]

The police certainly threatened to break his streak. Against the backdrop of the lady's silence (one editor dubbed her the "icy blonde"), investigators announced they knew why she had done it. They announced that Gebhardt had a wife and children in Germany. He could not have legally wed Vera. Moreover, forty-eight hours before the shooting, Dr. Gebhardt had a rendezvous with another blond at the Lincoln Hotel. The police had evidence that Vera had followed him to the hotel, registering in a room of her own under a false name, and she learned then that he had taken another mistress. It was a love murder. She killed him out of jealousy.

Such was the prosecution's picture of the case as Vera Stretz went on trial. She had to testify to save herself; she was a pitiful figure in the witness box. Well dressed, attractive, and tearful, she told the story of her complex relationship with the man she killed. Her attorney guided her through the details. "He told me that he loved me. And then he said that he was an unusual person. Ordinary laws applied to ordinary people, but for an unusual person there must be different standards. I . . . I was fascinated by him." When he refused to marry her, she had tried to break things off with him, she said. He responded by threatening her, throwing her on the bed, and raping her. He then asked her to perform an act of oral sex upon him that was so foreign to her, and so shameful, that she had been unable to tell the police. Now she told all, at the insistence of the judge, but only through violent, uncontrollable sobbing. She seized her gun, followed by a struggle for the gun, which "just went off" as they so often do in the hands of a woman who must defend herself from a man who demands such an unnatural sexual act as fellatio. But she shot him four times; this she explained by insisting that he fell on the bed with the initial shot, then got up and lunged again at her, so she had to shoot him again and again and again.

She was cross-examined for four hours. The prosecutor pointed out that the dead man's wounds were to his chest, back, and arm. The prosecutor tried to get her to admit she was in a hot fever of jealousy because Fritz wouldn't give up his wife and had a new mistress. But he could not trip up Vera Stretz.

Her attorney gave a closing argument for Vera that was studied then—for there were always countless attorneys in attendance whenever Samuel Leibowitz was at the podium—and is still studied today. Leibowitz initially focused on the victim. Fritz Gebhardt was actually a man of much accomplishment. It was unanimously agreed in the press that he was handsome, fascinating, cultured, highly intelligent, trilingual, and worldly. In World War I, he flew in the famous Richtofen Squadron. It was said he was very friendly during the war with another pilot, Hermann Goering. He had degrees from the University of Frankfurt in philosophy and political economy. Any political aspirations he may have harbored were quashed when he married a Jewish woman; he had left her in Germany with two children and no divorce. While living in New York, he had made half a million dollars brokering deals between German and American firms.

In Samuel Liebowitz's hands, this became the biography of a beast. "By the time the little Jewish lawyer had finished his closing address, Gebhardt had been transformed from wealthy German financier into Aryan monster, a closet Nazi, someone so perverted by sexual excess that shooting was too good for him."[3] His client, however, was a dignified woman. "Look at this poor girl," her attorney remarked. "Does she look like a honky-tonker? Does she look like a gold digger? Did Gebhardt ever give her a penny in his life? Did he ever pay her rent? She had thirty-five thousand dollars in her own right. . . . [She] is an educated woman, a woman of the world, but a 'sucker' for a man like that. What do we men know about love? What do we know anyhow about that complex bundle of nerves in the skull of the human species that we call woman? He whispers sweet nothings in her ears and she says in her heart, 'Why, this is love!'"

Leibowitz is widely lauded to this day as one of the great trial law-yers of American history and his closing in the Stretz case the apex of his remarkable career.[4] Following the defense's closing, Judge Corne-lius Collins gave his charge and instructions to the jury, which lasted an astonishing five hours. "If you believe her story," he finished acidly, "acquit her." They did, in three hours. The furious judge went to his chambers without thanking the jury.

The day after her acquittal, the freed killer met the press at her law-yer's office.

"Don't let this ruin your life," said a woman reporter.

"My life is ruined already," Vera replied. "I can never be the same woman again." She declared she was done with men; she would never be married or have a family. She intended to write her memoirs.[5] If she did, sadly, they were never published, and she vanished into obscurity.

COUNTESS
MARIE O'ROURKE
TARNOVSKA

"I here put up a sign warning the whole pestiferous crew of Pharisees to dive no deeper here. . . . There are women who are wantons by nature; whom no wealth, education, or moral surroundings can withhold from evil."

—Brann the Iconoclast, *The Common Courtesan*

THE VICTIM: Count Pavel Kamarovsky
WHEN: September 3, 1907
WHERE: Venice, Italy

THE CASE

Men who author books on female criminals sometimes cannot help but issue dire warnings (tinged with jealousy, if not possessiveness) aimed at new or casual students of the femme fatale. Those of us who can rationalize our interest in the most alluring daughters of Eve concede that studying this type of killer is an endeavor not to be lightly undertaken. A stroll through the gallery of the world's worst women exposes the disciple to a gauntlet of sirens who come from every culture and sing in every tongue known to humankind. Legions are the fatal ladies whose strange spells grow more intoxicating with time. Their bones are dust, but they have left us their portraits and photographs and in many cases reams of judicial transcripts that immortalize their sins for posterity. They are

Countess Tarnovska, who was accused of conspiring with two of her lovers to murder her fiancé for his life insurance policy. (*Photo by Topical Press Agency/ Getty Images*)

appealing and repulsive, bewitching and beastly, and if you pause too long before any one of them, she will enchant you.

If a woman's wickedness were measured by her social standing, the number of her victims, and the strength and longevity of her infamy, one fatal beauty would emerge as the worst femme fatale in all the recorded annals of the wickedness of womankind: Countess Marie Nicolaena O'Rourke Tarnovska. *Cave amantem.*

She was the Russian Delilah. Like the biblical heroine, she murdered by proxy. Her only weapons were her beauty and sex. With these, she orchestrated scenes worthy of Chekhov and led at least five men to their doom. When she was arrested for murder in Italy in 1907, the case caused an international stir. A special cable to the *Washington Post* declared that the investigation alone was enough to create "a greater sensation in Europe than any episode in the criminal history of the continent," featuring an accused who "looms up as the most beautiful and captivating queen of the great criminal adventuresses of history." The *New York Times* dubbed her "a beautiful woman who wrought more harm than any other of her generation" and "one of the most beguiling and bemusing of all the daughters of Kali" (in reference to the ferocious four-armed Hindu goddess legendary for slaughtering men). Added the *Indianapolis Star,* unpatriotically yielding the palm for producing the world's worst woman to the Russians: "America, with its Cassie Chadwicks, its daring adventuresses and its feminine soldiers of fortune, has never contained such a wonderful performer upon the heartstrings of mankind as this Russian countess. In the world of love and of intrigue the woman is a genius." An editor in Jamaica called her case the Crime That Thrills the World.

What made the trial of Countess Tarnovska (often spelled Tarnowska) particularly fascinating was that she was a flagrant psychopath whose torts were exposed on cross-examination while she stood in the dock before an astonished worldwide audience. In the decades since the verdict, spellbound admirers have devoured millions of books in a dozen languages about her case. On the one hundredth anniversary of the spectacle, the lawyers of Venice re-created her legendary trial in the original courtroom at St. Mark's, overlooking the Grand Canal.

It is not coincidental that the world's worst woman would emerge from a dying autocratic class. If Countess Tarnovska merrily trampled the hearts of men until she glimpsed too late the precipice, then Imperial Russian society during the Belle Époque was guilty of letting her sins go so far unchecked. The countess was a daughter of the Silver Age. Like the perfume she wore (*L'Origan* by Coty), her culture no longer exists. Born in 1877, she matured just as the aristocracy faced its end days. Even in the 1890s they referred to the coming revolution and governed themselves accordingly. Waves of suicides and scores of carnal scandals marked the waning days of the empire. Marriage as an institution collapsed, even though (or perhaps because) it was next to impossible to get a divorce in the tsar's Russia. Thus the doomed elite tried, as the historians put it, to "free themselves through exalted romantic and sexual liaisons." Russian society women (already known for shocking tourists with their cigarette smoking, décolletages, and lax attitudes toward marital fidelity) forgot their scruples entirely. The last empress publicly fretted over the fact, vowing to reform the morals of married ladies. Her campaign failed, and her court called her a boor. A good half of the women from the highest aristocratic class in Russia were said to be *demimondaines,* habitually adulterous. As an American diplomat observed, "Marriage is a mere matter of convenience. The master indulges his tastes, and the mistress gratifies her whims."[1] Countess Tarnovska would one day claim that bad company led her astray. If she had not been as deviant as she was, going far beyond what was conceivable even in the Silver Age, then her cultural defense might have succeeded.

When young, the countess was a typical Russian blue blood. She was the middle daughter of Colonel Count Nicholas O'Rourke, descendant of an Irish soldier of fortune who gained a title for military service to the House of Romanov. Marie grew up on a country estate outside Kiev and matured into a tall, classical beauty with a high shape ("the best figure in Europe," an editor would one day declare).[2] She was also known for her husky, low voice; the expressiveness of her large, heavy-lidded, Slavic eyes; the charm of her conversation; and her mastery of several languages.

With these attributes, Marie had her pick of men, and at age seventeen she met the unfortunate Count Vassili Tarnovsky. It was said that he was besotted with her from the moment his cousin Mikhail introduced them.[3] Their families both disapproved, but the two eloped soon after meeting. Marie was lucky to marry so well and so hastily. Count Tarnovsky was, when they met, a man of enormous wealth and a notable patron of the arts and antiquities. He was the heir to several prestigious properties, including a famous country estate known as Kachanovka Palace. For a while, on the arm of a handsome man her elder and better, Marie enjoyed society life in Moscow and Kiev, devoting herself to luxuries and pleasures. When in Kiev, they resided close to the Golden Gate, and in the countryside, they enjoyed days-long parties. They had two children in quick succession, Tatjana and Vassili Vassilovich, but their marital bliss was short-lived.

Marie took her first step on the path to eternal infamy as a new bride when she chose an obvious liaison. She had an affair with a sixteen-year-old student. He was also troubled, and she knew this. Moreover, he was Count Tarnovsky's younger brother, Peter Tarnovsky. For a woman who would one day become infamous for her "constantly deepening immorality," it was a fiendish beginning. It was said that she did it to fool her husband, to make him jealous, and to prove her superiority. She may well have done it just for the fun of the thing. When Peter hanged himself in 1898, some said it was because he failed his exams and feared his father. Others blamed the young enchantress for provoking him to suicide.[4]

Her adulterous appetites grew. Marie flaunted affairs before a shocked household staff and the rest of society. "There were many scandals," the papers would report, "concerning her relations with officers in her house." As her marriage dissolved, her children were sent to live with relatives. At the same time, the countess took up with a young medical student, Baron Vladimir Stahl. A sickly alcoholic, he became her devoted servant and introduced her to two new loves, morphine and cocaine. Marie demanded that he pledge his allegiance to her in writing, expressing her desire to dominate him and feed her vanity. He complied by sending many long love letters (which, once entered into evidence, would be deemed "extraordinary epistles"). "On my word of honor," he wrote in one, "and by all that remains strong and pure within me, I, Vladimir Stahl, promise Marie Nicolaevna Tarnovska to do all that she commands of me. . . . I shall always act in the name of that pure love which has already taken up the whole of my life. . . . Keeping this promise, I declare under oath that, save with the loss of my word of honor, Countess Tarnovska shall be sacred and inviolable to me."

The countess was visiting Dr. Stahl for more of what she craved when, in 1898, she attracted the notice of another of the doctor's visitors. He was a handsome officer named Alexis Bozevsky. Marie was haughty and ignored him. In so doing, she smited him. Both memorialized their affair in graphic correspondence. The "Marquise" de Sade tested Bozevsky as the tsar's army never had, and he proved an apt pupil. She declared him inconstant. He vowed he would prove how much he loved her. He would let her shoot him with his own weapon. He offered the palm of his hand and invited her to put a bullet through it. Marie raised the barrel. She fired. Then she raised his bloody hand to her lips and kissed the wound.

There are many accounts of what happened next. The scene has been fictionalized in several settings. The most reliable sources indicate that Count Tarnovsky caught his wife and her lover Bozevsky in flagrante delicto. What is not disputed is that Tarnovsky retrieved a weapon and shot Alexis Bozevsky.

Marie fled their home with her wounded lover. She called on their mutual friend, Dr. Vladimir Stahl, to tend him. Instead, Stahl and the countess made love on a couch near the sick man's bed. When they awoke from their drug-addled play, Bozevsky was dead.

Count Tarnovsky was arrested for murder. The mandatory punishment should he be convicted was death. When he went on trial for his life, he enriched the coffers of newspaper publishers across Russia. But he drained his family's assets. The Tarnovskys were forced to sell Kachanovka Palace to fund his defense to the murder charge. But in the end, another Unwritten Rule—that universal legal principle positing that a man who catches his wife in the arms of another has the right to take lethal action to avenge his honor—resulted in Count Tarnovsky's acquittal. After that harrowing ordeal, Tarnovsky filed for divorce. It would mean yielding another sizeable portion of his fortune to his wife. He would also lose his place in his regiment—not because he killed a man, but because divorced men were forced to resign in disgrace. At that point, neither he nor his wife had any reputation left to protect. Both were ruined.

Alexis Bozevsky was barely cold when Marie lost another lover. Dr. Stahl took poison, penned one last love letter to the countess, and breathed his last for a woman who had already found yet another lover to replace him.

Donat Prilukov of Moscow was an experienced attorney and had made a fine living as an advocate of the law. He had an exceptional mind. Unlike 98 percent of Russian lawyers, Prilukov was not of noble blood. He was an entirely self-made and successful man. Then he met *La Tarnovska*.

Marie called him her *mugik*, her peasant. She also called him "The Scorpion." Some would say the brilliant lawyer preyed on a weak-willed woman, making her his tool. Others painted a picture of a "fond lover anxious to deliver her from her unhappy marriage." Prilukov's legal secretary, Mr. Smaiefsky, would one day testify that the lawyer was a model of integrity until he became violently infatuated with Countess Tarnovska. He hired detectives to learn everything he could about her. When she saw other men, he learned of it and, to her delight, threw jealous tantrums. Marie met in Donat a man who was her moral equal. Water seeks its own level. He left his family and abandoned his law practice to devote himself completely to her. Marie forbade him from seeing his wife and children. She also goaded him into doing acts that made him look ridiculous. At the theater one night, she talked him into jumping from their box onto the stage. Cigarettes featured prominently in what Marie called their "love play," as she enjoyed slowly destroying him. He lavished her with his personal fortune. When his personal funds ran dry, Prilukov misappropriated a fortune from his clients, reported to be close to 100,000 francs.

At that point, the pair decided to embark on a whirlwind tour of the continental capitals and resorts. The countess and her lawyer spent the spring of 1906 at the Grand Hotel in Vienna, where they stayed under false names. They also traveled in France and stayed in the best hotels in Berlin. Life on the lam must have been intoxicating for them until she spent almost all of his clients' trust accounts. Even beautiful Russian countesses must pay their hotel bills. They argued over the last four thousand. Finally the fatal countess gave up on her ruined lover, abandoning Donat Prilukov in Germany and returning to Russia alone.

In Orel, near Kiev, she met Count Pavel Kamarovsky, a wealthy widower who sported white linen suits and headed the Anti-Revolutionary League for the Russian monarch. They were inseparable in Orel. There she also met a friend of the count, a young, dreamy medical student named Nicholas Naumov. She learned that Nicholas enjoyed being beaten and took him for yet another lover. His previous mistress had let him run naked behind her carriage in the dust. An excited Marie indulged Nicholas and burned his arms and shoulders with her cigarettes. She stuck pins in his body, tattooing her name into his arm and rubbing *L'Origan* into each little wound. In his ecstasy, Nicholas Naumov forgot all about his studies and his wife and children. He gave up his life to be by her side.

But Marie grew bored, and her mind returned to her attorney in exile. Soon she was in a tearful reunion at a train station in Munich with Donat Prilukov. She regaled her lover with the details of her sexual adventures during their separation. He was insane with jealousy. She left him in Germany again, insistent on going back to her wealthy Count Kamarovsky. It was the count's turn to abandon his family and career to escort Marie around Europe.

In many cities they were shadowed by her other lovers, Prilukov and Naumov. She managed all three affairs dexterously, even eliciting a marriage proposal and an engagement party from her wealthy devotee, until the day came when she tired of Count Pavel Kamarovsky. She preferred Donat. The Scorpion had no money. She tried to extract what she could from her count, but wealthy men do not walk around with their money in their pockets. So she pleaded with him to consider the dangers to his life engendered by his politically sensitive position with the Anti-Revolutionary League. They struck a bargain: if Count Pavel Kamarovsky would insure his life for half a million francs, she would marry him on September 18, 1907, in Venice.

Kamarovsky traveled ahead to Venice to await her, taking rooms at the Campo Santa Maria del Giglio (now known as the Hotel Ala).[5] Days before the wedding, the count was found with a fatal gunshot wound to the abdomen. He identified his killer as his friend Nicholas Naumov.

Naumov was arrested, and instead of killing himself as promised, he confessed almost at once. "Paul [Pavel] was a brute, and I, myself, was in love with Marie." A search of his room revealed letters from the countess and her attorney, and the entire scheme unraveled.

At long last, Marie had brought about a man's death in a manner that was specifically prohibited by the criminal codes. Something in her careful plans had gone awry. She was arrested on suspicion of murder. In her own trunk was much of the evidence that would be used against her: cocaine, pornography, love letters, telegrams, a whip made of willow branches that she used to beat Nicholas, and a collection of suicide notes from some of her dead lovers. The correspondence revealed that Marie had conspired with two of her lovers to kill her fiancé. The plan was supposed to end with the arrest, confession, and suicide of Nicholas Naumov, but Nicholas had failed to kill himself after he shot the count.

Almost from the moment of the countess's arrest, the experts knew that the titled beauty was an extraordinary specimen—a true femme fatale. During the initial criminal proceedings for the countess, a prosecutor assigned to the case to question her had to be removed from his assignment. He had fallen in love with the defendant.

Countess Tarnovska's case was one of the last to be the object of study and comment by world-famous Italian criminologist and author Dr. Cesare Lombroso. Though he did not live to see her trial, he perused the evidence elicited at an early inquest. He believed Marie Tarnovska was perfectly sane and probably guilty of conspiracy to commit an insurance murder. In a written report, he concluded: "If the Countess actually conceived, planned, and carried out the tragedy. . . . then she is the most remarkable criminal of modern times. Her methods show an absolute mastery of masculine sentiment, passion, and covetousness. The crimes of the Borgias and of the *Strozzi* offer no parallels. Her antecedents must have been very remarkable, for it is unusual for one of criminal proclivities to plan so rational a conspiracy. . . . She is absolutely original."

The trial of Countess Tarnovska, Donat Prilukov, and Nicholas Naumov for the murder of Pavel Kamarovsky was perhaps the hottest indoor ticket in the history of Venice. Reporters, lawyers, artists, world-famous actresses, and even noblemen vied for seats to witness the testimony of

Countess Tarnovska enters the courthouse on April 3, 1910. (Photographer: Philipp Kester. Published by: 'Berliner Illustrirte Zeitung' 12/1910. Vintage property of ullstein bild [Photo by Philipp Kester/ullstein bild via Getty Images.])

a Muse who killed without compunction and whose battlefields were ballrooms. When pressed to explain their presence in the Venetian courtroom, they readily confessed their "fascination with Tarnovska."[6] Sensational novelist and playwright Gabriele d'Annunzio sat next to Parisian novelist Madame Daniel Lesueur. Following with great interest, d'Annunzio announced he was writing a piece based on *La Tarnovska* (as the French called her), and some large European theaters were already asking for the finished play. Prince Luigi, Duke of Abruzzi, and Princess Odescalchi were in the gallery. It was the first time in living memory that a prince and princess of the blood could be found in the audience at a murder trial. Edgar Degas, the French sculptor and painter famous for his portraits of dancers, attended with the intention of using the defendant for a model. The "Siren of the Adriatic" also drew a flock of actresses to the courthouse. Sarah Bernhardt, the great tragedienne and most famous actress of her age, kept her name in the headlines by attending trials in which she spotted a future dramatic role for herself. She was present for much of the Tarnovska trial, along with her Italian rival Emma Gramatica and French stage legend Gabrielle Réjane. British author Baron Corvo was another who came to hear for himself what the newspapers could not publish. He summoned only a single word to describe it: "Amazing!"

Naumov, pawn of a black-hearted queen, gave his testimony first. "She cast the spell of her terrible eyes over me and made me her slave," he stated. "I feared her, yet she fascinated me. I tried to avoid her, but wherever she went I was destined to follow. A power I could not resist drew me to her. She planned all the hideous details of murder and made me swear on her own mother's grave that I would carry the plan into action.

"Sometimes she extinguished her cigarettes by pressing them against my hand and burning the flesh. At others she ran the point of a dagger over me. But she charmed and fascinated me. I loved her, and when she ordered me to kill a man I knew to be innocent, I had to obey."

"But why," Naumov was asked, "did she want him killed?"

"It was to avenge her honor."

"Well, your honor was not concerned."

"No, but I was her slave. Also, I was jealous of the Count."

"Why was that?"

"Because an officer at Orel told me he had once seen him leaving the Countess's bedroom in very scanty attire. He said it was not the correct costume for a mere friendly visit to a lady. This displeased me."

"But—and I am compelled to put the question—did you resume your relations with her after this episode?"

"That is the case."

"You have a forgiving temperament!"

The court read a telegram Naumov had sent Marie: "I know where this man lives. I abominate and detest him. Whatever happens I will set you free."

And another: "Body and soul, I belong to my adored Marie. I weep for our broken happiness."

And then the forged telegram that Donat Prilukov sent to Marie Tarnovska, which she passed on to Naumov to inflame him: "I know all. Naumov is a cad, and you are good for nothing. I regret my sentiments for you. Paul Kamarovsky."

Asked the court: "What were this woman's last words to you, as you left for Venice?"

"She said, 'Now I know that you really love me.'"

Donat Prilukov was the next to testify. He told the court he was dominated by the countess. When they met, he was a happy husband and father, a respected attorney, a professional. He repeatedly tried to break with Marie, but she controlled him, he said. "She was too strong for me. There was nothing I would not have done at her command. Because she wished it, I left my wife. I robbed my clients. I sacrificed my honor. And once I even tried to kill myself."

"Yes, and you also tried to kill Count Kamarovsky. That is the matter before us at this moment."

"It was not my wish. As I have told you, I was in love with the Countess. We both considered that Naumov would be the best man to do the job."

"We have here a telegram forwarded to you in Venice by the prisoner Tarnovska. It says, 'Berta's decision to educate Adele is very serious.' What does this mean?"

"It is a code message. What is means is Naumov has decided to kill Kamarovsky."

"And this one: 'Berta prefers a hot dish.' Is that also in code?"

"Of course it is. It means Naumov will use a revolver."

Marie Tarnovska then stood in the dock. A judge ordered the blinds pulled up at the request of photographers who wanted to better illuminate her face. The countess, cloaked in black, lifted her veil and stood pale and trembling before a courtroom packed to suffocation. She noticed her father in his military uniform. Upon seeing him, she burst into tears.

The prosecuting attorney fiercely questioned her for hours about the apex of her stunning career, the murder plot that was so complex some would say she elevated the double cross to a fine art.[7] He then went beyond the charges to ask her about her connections with other tragedies. Inside the courtroom, the questioning heightened an atmosphere already electric with excitement.

"Kamarovsky telegraphed to you twice as he was lying in the hospital dying, calling you to his side?"

"But I telegraphed." (Her message to her dying fiancé had read: "Am terribly upset at what has happened. I love you and am in despair that I cannot come to you.")

"It is said that before your divorce you excited your husband against your lovers and your lovers against your husband so as to provoke a duel and get rid of your husband."

"False—absolutely false. My husband fought a duel with Tolstoy for another woman."

"Prilukov too says that you gave yourself up to your brother-in-law, in order to excite him to remorse and urge him to suicide. Is that so? Answer!"

"Good heavens! He was only a child of sixteen." When pressed, she added bitterly, "You know I was accused of causing that suicide."

Was it true that she had a passion for Alexis Bozevsky?

"I yielded to him," she admitted. "In doing so, I admit I was wrong. But I found him kind and affectionate, when the man I had married was cruel and neglectful. A woman wants love. Alexis gave it to me. Vassili withheld it."

"He was your first lover?"

"He was the only one among them all who really appealed to me."

"Prilukov has told us that you had many lovers, and that among them was a Monsieur Zolatariev."

"Then it is idiotic of him to say so."

"Why?"

"Because this man was old and ugly, and hadn't a ruble to bless himself with."

"And what about Doctor Stahl, who committed suicide for your sake?"

"Not for my sake. Please be accurate, whatever else you are. Vladimir killed himself because he quarreled with his wife."

"Listen to this letter from him," the prosecutor said. "'Dear Marie Nicolaenva. Instead of at five o'clock, I arrived at the anatomical theatre at nine o'clock. I shall live for forty minutes more. All is ended. My love for you lives. I kiss you and I die.'"

The prosecutor asked, "Have you anything to say to that?"

"Surely I am not responsible if men do foolish things."

"How did you first meet Naumov?"

"Kamarovsky introduced me at Orel."

"Were you in love with him?"

"Yes, I was."

"And what were your relations with Kamarovsky and Prilukov at this period?"

"They were tender."

"So it would appear, Madame. What, however, is not so clear is why you should want three lovers simultaneously?"

"It was because I was endeavoring to find somebody who would really love me. Instead, I was always deluded. Nobody corresponded with my ideal."

"Yet you allowed each of these three men to think you would marry him?"

"Ah, but the engagement was not official."

She could not deny what was obvious to every onlooker. The countess herself made it clear that she was guilty of the charges leveled against her, all but confessing to her role in many tragedies. Countess Marie Tarnovska was exposed by wide-ranging, unchecked, withering cross-examination as a narcissistic psychopath as she declared, "I am the most unfortunate woman in the world. I am a martyr to my own beauty. For any man to behold me is for him to love me. The whole pathway of my life is strewn with the bodies of those who loved me most." Like every femme fatale before and since, this woman with countless lovers proved that she was a woman to be pitied for having no heart at all. She was incapable of truly loving a man or of sustaining any genuine relationship with any one of them. Her promiscuity and her need to inflict pain on her lovers was merely the perverse expression of her frustrations and of her driving need to find a man who was smart enough and strong enough to dominate her. Her challenge was that she despised the men who fell in love with her so much that she *preferred* them dead, and die they did because she wished it.

And yet, such was her hypnotic power over men that a member of the jury had to be taken off the case after Marie Tarnovska testified. He was in love with the accused and could no longer hide it. For her remarkable ability to enchant a man with her courtroom appearance alone, *while being publicly denounced* for her crimes against men, *La Tarnovska* is unequaled as a femme fatale, the best of the worst.

With the support of her wealthy father, the countess mounted an expensive defense. A score of medical experts took the stand, including surgeons, alienists, and gynecologists, many of them noted in their field: Redlich, Fenomenof, Rhein, Professor Bossi, Professor Berri, Professor Eugenio Tanzi, Dr. Mennini. For days on end, they declared that the countess was merely the victim of a feminine disorder. If it weren't for this disease, she would have been an angel of goodness. Onlookers were not convinced that Tarnovska's flaws were gynecological in nature. "That she was born with a kink in her brain is evident," as one trial observer remarked. The odds were against her in the betting on the outcome.

The jury indeed convicted the countess. But they found by a bare majority that she suffered from a "partial mental infirmity." Her sentence for inciting her lovers to murder was eight years, with two years of credit for time served. Her lawyer, Donat Prilukov, was also convicted, but the jury found no mitigating infirmity in the case of the attorney. The judges sentenced Prilukov to ten years in prison.

As to the actual gunman, the jury found that Nicholas Naumov intended to murder Count Kamarovsky while under mental impairment. That he was the dupe of his dangerous mistress was proven beyond a doubt. The jury found that Countess Tarnovska instigated and incited Naumov to murder. Though Naumov was found guilty of the *actus reus* of killing of the count, the judges deemed him the least accountable. He was sentenced to time served. Before he departed the courtroom, Naumov turned to the countess, bent over her hand, and kissed it. The newspapers objected and the public was incensed by the light sentences. Per one observer, "Severe criticisms were heard on every hand." It was one final scandal to conclude one of the most shocking murder trials in history.

The lawyer who evoked the harshest punishment repeatedly tried to kill himself in prison—first by strangulation, then by poison, then by hanging. He eventually succeeded in opening his veins. Donat Prilikov was at least the fifth man to die for the countess, if one also counted Peter Tarnovsky, Alexis Bozevsky, Vladimir Stahl, and Pavel Kamarovsky.

When the prison gates finally swung open for Marie Tarnovska in 1915, the Romanov Dynasty verged on collapse as hunger spread through Russia and millions of men died in pointless wars of empire. She never returned to her homeland. The Venus of Venice slipped into obscurity. It is not quite known where she went or when she died because the rumors disagree. The most credible is that she moved to Paris, where she met an American who took her to South America. Many think she passed away in Santa Fe, Argentina, in 1945.

According to some of the literature on personality disorders, psychopaths can improve with time and experience. Most experts think not. One would hope that no other man lost his life for loving the world's most prolific femme fatale.

† † †

For more information: Hans Habe, *The Countess* (international bestseller in numerous editions and languages, 1963).

EPILOGUE

The Femme Fatale Lives

> Laura is convinced that a pretty face has tipped the scales of justice when Rob—on jury duty—sides with the attractive defendant.
> —Plot of the *Dick Van Dyke Show,* March 1962

Women across the world have actually been acquitted in seemingly clear-cut cases of premeditated strangulation, poisoning, shooting, and stabbing based on their good looks alone, as I have been trying to prove to you since page one. The rule applies to women particularly, and to particularly beautiful women, sometimes even in a case of first-degree murder. Take each of the cases in this collection and reverse the genders; we can only imagine what would happen to a *man* who committed an identical act. Could anyone imagine a man shooting an unarmed woman and then claiming he was suicidal and they were struggling for the gun and gosh it just went off—and getting away with it?

In most of these cases, the femme fatale was misjudged by a jury made up solely of men. It is beyond discouraging to think that men who were painstakingly vetted in voir dire and elevated to a position to pass judgment on a woman for criminal behavior simply could not bring themselves to set aside the sex element and judge her impartially. This is pitiful.

If grown, responsible male citizens cannot set aside their sex-related biases in the context of administering criminal justice under the gravest of circumstances, when *can* they?

Cartoonist: Jonny Hawkins. (www. CartoonStock.com.)

"I'm afraid I'll have to sentence you to five years, but you've been a <u>beautiful</u> defendant."

If men cannot set aside their male biases on behalf of a murder victim, for crying out loud, what do you suppose has happened in the routine drunk driving prosecutions or shoplifting trials at your local courthouse?

We can't simply blame men for this phenomenon, however. Women have now demonstrated that they will also grant preferential treatment to the good-looking defendant. Otherwise the advent of coed juries at the beginning of the twentieth century would have ended the presumption in favor of the attractive. It did not. Women have served on juries in the Western world for a good century now, yet the bias is still in play. We now know that acquitting pretty women who do not deserve leniency is not a male prerogative, and men are not wholly to blame. We continue to see this phenomenon in American and European jurisprudence (and far beyond, I'd wager, if we were to break down language barriers). When Susan Cummings was tried in 1997 in Virginia, her attorney sought women for the jury, and his gambit succeeded; the female jurors wept in response to her "woe is me" defense.[1] American

Amanda Knox was convicted in Italy of murdering her roommate Meredith Kercher in 2007 but four years later was cleared of all charges. Without taking any position on her complicated case, whether guilty or not, if Amanda Knox had not been very beautiful, she never would have gotten the worldwide attention that ultimately saw her set free.

The Beauty Defense cannot be shrugged off as a historical phenomenon, an aberration, a fluke peculiar to all-male panels. A random assortment of a dozen citizens, otherwise known as a jury, is as unreliable now as it has always been, be they male, female, or mixed, and jurors of any gender tend to attribute to pretty people more warmth and character than they actually have. Our modern sociologists have now scientifically proven the existence of the unspoken preference for attractive people by conducting experiments with mock juries made up presumably of men and women of moral lives. Their objective findings are no surprise to those who know the unwritten laws. "When the defendant was attractive, judgment shifted toward acquittal, but when the defendant was unattractive, there was no such shift. As a result, mock juries were more likely to acquit the attractive defendant."[2]

Since we have examples from our current century, we can say that beauty remains a viable defense for any would-be killer who abides by certain cautions, and we can never stop fearing the femme fatales who live and kill among us. *Cave amantem.*

NOTES

INTRODUCTION

1. *Lex non scripta* is a Latin phrase meaning an unwritten law.

2. The expression first appears in 1615 in the work of French historian Jean de Serres in his *Inventaire général de l'histoire de France*. The first woman ever dubbed a femme fatale was Queen Elizabeth. In 1710, French author Charles Cotolendi called her such in his book *Saint-Evremoniana,* referring to her treatment of the handsome-until-headless Count of Essex.

3. Xenophon and Josiah Renick Smith, *Memorabilia* (New York: Arno Press, 1979.

4. Wolfgang Lederer, *The Fear of Women* (New York: Grune & Stratton, 1968).

5. Inez Calloway Cobb, in "The New York Woman," *Associated Press,* Nov. 13, 1936.

6. John Pemberton, *Myths and Legends: From Cherokee Dances to Voodoo Trances* (New York: Chartwell Books, 2010).

7. For more on Phryne (and some of her sisters in infamy), see Henry Lilienheim, *The Most Interesting Women of All Time* (Montreal, QC: DLI Productions, 2001).

8. With a nod to Edmund L. Pearson and his essay "Rules for Murderesses," in Edmund Lester Pearson, *Instigation of the Devil. [Being Veracious Accounts of Twenty or Thirty Murders and Other Odd Occurrences]* (New York: Charles Scribner's Sons, 1930).

9. Jay Robert Nash, *Look for the Woman* (New York: M. Evans, 1981).

10. Maurine Watkins and Thomas H. Pauly, *Chicago: With the* Chicago Tribune *Articles That Inspired It* (Carbondale: Southern Illinois Univ. Press, 1997).

11. James Lough, "Why Juries Never Convict Pretty Women," *Washington Post,* May 9, 1915.

12. 57 *Ohio Law Bulletin* 510, "Women Jurors to Try Feminine Murders" (Norwalk: Ohio Law Bulletin, 1912).

13. Douglas Perry, *The Girls of Murder City* (London: Penguin, 2011).

14. Quentin Reynolds, *The Story of Samuel S. Leibowitz* (New York: Farrer, Straus and Co., 1950).

15. Virginia Rounding, *Grandes Horizontales: The Lives and Legends of Marie Duplessis, Cora Pearl, La Paiva, and La Presidente* (New York: Bloomsbury, 2004).

16. Paul Spicer, *The Temptress: The Scandalous Life of Alice de Janzé and the Mysterious Death of Lord Erroll* (New York: St. Martin's Griffin, 2011).

17. Laura James, *The Love Pirate and the Bandit's Son: Murder, Sin, and Scandal in the Shadow of Jesse James* (New York: Union Square Press, 2009).

18. Lisa Appignanesi, *Trials of Passion: Crimes in the Name of Love and Madness* (London: Virago, 2016).

19. French: a beautiful lady without mercy.

20. Reynolds, *The Story of Samuel S. Leibowitz.*

21. L. Kay Gillespie, *Dancehall Ladies: Executed Women of the 20th Century* (Lanham, MD: Univ. Press of America, 2000).

22. Kathleen A. Cairns, *Proof of Guilt: Barbara Graham and the Politics of Executing Women in America* (Lincoln: Univ. of Nebraska Press, 2013).

23. Darla Pugh, *Psycho Chick: The True Story of Penny Bjorkland* (Scotts Valley, CA: CreateSpace, 2016).

24. Perry, *Girls of Murder City.*

25. Linda Stunnell, *Women out of Control* (New York: Carroll & Graf, 2007).

26. Sarah Stillman, "Foxy Knoxy: Sex, Violence and Media Hysteria," CNN.com, http://globalpublicsquare.blogs.cnn.com/2011/10/05/foxy-knoxy-sex-violence-and-media-hysteria/.

27. In 1551, Mrs. Arden murdered her husband Thomas Arden of Faversham with the help of her lover. She was burned at the stake. The case has inspired numerous works of fiction.

28. Katharine Nairn fell in love with her husband's brother, and the pair conspired to murder her husband with arsenic. Katharine was tried, convicted, and sentenced to death, but she escaped before the sentence could be carried out. See William Roughead, *Trial of Katharine Nairn* (Toronto: Canada Law Book Co., 1926).

29. Bathsheba Spooner murdered her husband with the help of her lover and was executed despite the fact that she was pregnant. See Deborah Navas, *Murdered by His Wife* (Amherst: Univ. of Massachusetts Press, 1999).

30. John Kobler, *The Trial of Ruth Snyder and Judd Gray* (Garden City, NY: Doubleday, Doran & Co., 1938).

31. Kerry Segrave, *Women and Capital Punishment in America, 1840–1899* (Jefferson, NC: McFarland & Co., 2008).

32. Charles M. Hargroder, *Ada and the Doc: An Account of the Ada LeBoeuf-Thomas Dreher Murder Case* (Lafayette: Center for Louisiana Studies, Univ. of Louisiana at Lafayette, 2000).

33. Laura Thompson, *Rex v. Edith Thompson: A Tale of Two Murders* (London: Head of Zeus, 2018).

34. Mark Gado, *Death Row Women: Murder, Justice, and the New York Press* (Westport, CT: Praeger Publishers, 2008).

35. Tony Thorne, *Countess Dracula* (London: Bloomsbury, 1997).

36. Interestingly, fiction based on true crime preceded the invention of the newspaper in 1666. "As early as 1592, we find in *Arden of Feversham* an English drama closely patterned on the lurid facts of a family murder, and its progeny have been countless. An attempt to survey the immense debt of theatre and fiction to crime history. . . . would be beyond the reach of bibliography, not to mention literary analysis." Albert Borowitz, *A Gallery of Sinister Perspectives: Ten Crimes and a Scandal* (Kent, OH: Kent State Univ. Press, 1982).

37. Elizabeth Jenkins, *Six Criminal Women* (Freeport, NY: Books for Libraries Press, 1971).

38. Anne Somerset, *Unnatural Murder: Poison at the Court of James I* (London: Weidenfeld & Nicolson, 2017).

39. Brian Vallée, *The Torso Murder: The Untold Story of Evelyn Dick* (Toronto: Key Porter Books, 2001).

40. Kori Mayer, *Black Widow: The True Story of Louise Peete* (Scotts Valley, CA: CreateSpace, 2015).

41. James C. Hays, *I'm Just an Ordinary Girl: The Sharon Kinne Story* (Leatherwood, KS: Leathers Publ., 1997).

42. "Josephine Gray, Serial Killer of 3 Husbands by Proxy," unknownmisandry. blogspot.com, http://unknownmisandry.blogspot.com/2011/09/josephine-gray-serial -killer-of-3.html.

43. The story is probably best told in fiction in *The Paradine Case* by Robert Smith Hichens, an account of a happily married London lawyer who falls in love with the accused poisoner he defends on a murder charge, retold in the Hitchcock film of the same name.

44. Minott Saunders, "What the Paris Criminologists Have Learned about Love Murders," *Modesto News-Herald,* May 23, 1931.

45. James, *The Love Pirate and the Bandit's Son.*

46. John D. Lawson, *American State Trials*, vol. 17 (St. Louis, MO: Thomas Law Books, 1936). See also *Official Report of the Trial of Mary Harris, Indicted for the Murder of Adoniram J. Burroughs, before the Supreme Court of the District of Columbia (Sitting as a Criminal Court), Monday, July 3, 1865* (Washington, DC: W. H. & O. H. Morrison, undated).

47. Bill Neal, *Sex, Murder, and the Unwritten Law: Courting Judicial Mayhem, Texas Style* (Lubbock: Texas Tech Univ. Press, 2009); Gordon Bakken, *Women Who Kill Men: California Courts, Gender, and the Press* (Lincoln: Univ. of Nebraska Press, 2012).

48. Jeffrey S. Adler, "I Loved Joe, but I Had to Shoot Him: Homicide by Women in Turn-of-the-Century Chicago," *Journal of Criminal Law and Criminology* 92 (2001–2): 867–98.

BEULAH ANNAN

1. Adler, "I Loved Joe, but I Had to Shoot Him."

2. Perry, *Girls of Murder City.*

3. Colin Evans, *The Valentino Affair: The Jazz Age Murder Scandal That Shocked New York Society and Gripped the World* (Guilford, CT: Lyons Press, 2014).

4. Isabelle Patricola, "Hula Lou" (1923).

5. Watkins and Pauly, *Chicago.*

ELVIRA BARNEY

1. Giles Playfair, *Six Studies in Hypocrisy* (London: Secker & Warburg, 1969).

2. Elvira is often compared to Ruth Ellis, another party girl–turned-shootist. But Miss Ellis was at the opposite end of the class spectrum and had far too many lovers in evidence to come into compliance with the rules for murderesses. Ruth Ellis had the misfortune of being the last woman hanged in England. See Robert Hancock, *Ruth Ellis: The Last Woman to Be Hanged* (London: Orion, 2000).

3. Peter Cotes, *The Trial of Elvira Barney* (Newton Abbot, UK: David and Charles, 1976).

4. "Mystery of the Chinese Treasure behind the Society Cocktail Tragedy," *Hamilton (ON) Evening Journal,* Aug. 27, 1932.

5. Sir Travis Humphreys, *A Book of Trials* (London: Pan Books Ltd., 1956).

6. Edgar Lustgarten, "Modern Suite for Strings: Patrick Hastings Defends Elvira Barney," in *Defender's Triumph* (London: Wingate, 1951), 144–85.

7. Sir Patrick Hastings, *Cases in Court* (London: Pan Books, 1953).

ADELAIDE BARTLETT

1. Richard Daniel Altick, *Victorian Studies in Scarlet: Murders and Manners in the Age of Victoria* (New York: W. W. Norton, 1970).

2. F. Tennyson Jesse, *Murder and Its Motives* (London: G. G. Harrap, 1952).

3. Altick, *Victorian Studies in Scarlet.*

4. Yseult Bridges, *Poison and Adelaide Bartlett: The Pimlico Poisoning Case* (London: Hutchinson & Co., 1962).

5. See Albert Borowitz, "M. Tullius Cicero for the Defense," in *Innocence and Arsenic: Studies in Crime and Literature* (New York: Harper & Row, 1977), 100–115.

6. The full transcript was published after the trial and is one of the best trial transcripts ever published. Edward Beal, *Notable British Trials: The Trial of Adelaide Bartlett for Murder* (London: Stevens and Haynes, 1886). For more on Sir Clarke, see Sir Edward Clarke, *Selected Speeches* (London: Smith, Elder, 1908).

7. Edgar Lustgarten, "Victorian Trumpets: Edward Clarke Defends Adelaide Bartlett," in *Defender's Triumph* (New York: Scribner, 1951), 8–80.

8. Edward Wilfrid Fordham, *Notable Cross-Examinations* (London: Constable & Co., 1951); H. M. Walbrook, *Murders and Murder Trials 1812–1912* (London: Constable & Co., 1932).

9. This statement was true. Chloroform is very rare as a poison, and only a handful of cases are known to this day. One of note: H. H. Holmes used chloroform to kill his friend Benjamin Pitezel.

10. William Roughead, "The Luck of Adelaide Bartlett: A Fireside Tale," in *The Rebel Earl and Other Studies* (Edinburgh: W. Green & Son, 1926), 215–52.

COUNTESS LINDA MURRI BONMARTINI

1. Christina Vella, *Indecent Secrets: The Infamous Murri Murder Affair* (New York: Free Press, 2006).
2. "An Italian Tragedy," *New York Times,* June 13, 1909.
3. Nash, *Look for the Woman.*
4. Horace Wyndham, *Crime on the Continent* (Boston: Little, Brown, 1928).
5. Vella, *Indecent Secrets.*

KITTY BYRON

1. Neil R. A. Bell, Trevor N. Bond, Kate Clarke, and M. W. Oldridge, *The A–Z of Victorian Crime* (Stroud, UK: Amberley Publishing, 2016).
2. *Old Bailey Proceedings Online* (www.oldbaileyonline.org, version 7.2, Jan. 30, 2018), Dec. 1902, trial of EMMA BYRON (twenty-four), otherwise KITTY BYRON (t19021215–94).
3. Elizabeth Hennessy, "The Stock Exchange Murder," in *Coffee House to Cyber Market: 200 Years of the London Stock Exchange* (London: Ebury, 2001), 91.
4. Humphreys, *A Book of Trials.*
5. John Carter Wood, *The Most Remarkable Woman in England: Poison, Celebrity and the Trials of Beatrice Pace* (Manchester: Manchester Univ. Press, 2012).
6. Robert Jackson, *Case for the Prosecution: A Biography of Sir Archibald Bodkin, Director of Public Prosecutions, 1920–1930* (London: A. Barker, 1962).
7. Wood, *The Most Remarkable Woman in England.*

FLORENCE CARMAN

1. *Joplin (MO) Globe,* Oct. 22, 1914.
2. Evans, *The Valentino Affair.*
3. Nixola Greeley-Smith, "Is It Worth While to Put Women on Trial for Murder?," *Syracuse (NY) Herald,* Dec. 3, 1917.
4. Alex E. Sweet, "Gotham Juries the Most Unreliable Thing in the World," *Freeborn County Standard,* Sept. 9, 1891.

JESSIE COSTELLO

1. Sydney Horler, *Malefactors' Row: A Book of Crime Studies* (London: Robert Hale Ltd., 1940).
2. Edmund L. Pearson and Gerald Gross, eds., "Mrs. Costello Cleans the Boiler," in *Masterpieces of Murder* (Boston: Little, Brown and Co., 1963), 149–56.
3. Famous journalist Dorothy Kilgallen covered the case as her first jury trial. The reporter's freshman scoop was an exclusive interview with Jessie

Costello's lover that ran as a series in the *Boston Evening Journal.* John Jakes, *Great Women Reporters* (New York: G. P. Putnam's Sons, 1969).

4. Edward J. McMahon, *Uncensored Testimony of the "Cop" Who Kissed and Told: Costello Murder Trial* (Lynn, MA: N.p., 1933).

5. Pearson and Gross, *Masterpieces of Murder.*

6. Wood, *The Most Remarkable Woman in England.*

7. Lowell Ames Norris, "Who Killed Captain Costello?," *True Detective* (Jan. 1934).

8. Jakes, *Great Women Reporters.*

9. *Ophidian* means snake-like.

SUSAN CUMMINGS

1. Lisa Pulitzer, *A Woman Scorned: The Shocking Real-Life Case of Billion- airess Killer Susan Cummings* (New York: St. Martin's Press, 1999).

2. Lorena Bobbitt's case arose in 1993, when Lorena severed her husband's penis while he slept, earning headlines such as THE MANASSAS MUTILATION. At trial, she claimed her act was prompted by temporary insanity after her husband raped her. She was acquitted. See Alan M. Dershowitz, *The Abuse Excuse: And Other Cop-outs, Sob Stories, and Evasions of Responsibility* (Boston: Little, Brown and Co., 1994).

GERMAINE D'ANGLEMONT

1. Theodore Zeldin, *A History of French Passions, 1848–1945* (Oxford: Oxford Univ. Press, 1977).

2. French: a husband who acquiesces to his wife's adultery.

3. Nigel West, *Historical Dictionary of World War I Intelligence* (Lanham, MD: Rowman & Littlefield Pub., 2014).

4. French: women of the half-world; promiscuous hedonists financially supported by their lovers; in some contexts, courtesans or prostitutes.

5. Sarah Maza, *Violette Noziere: A Story of Murder in 1930s Paris* (Berkeley: Univ. of California Press, 2011).

6. French: five to seven, the hours conducive to after-work adultery.

7. French: a lover's tryst.

8. Janet Flanner, "Murder among the Lovebirds," *Vanity Fair,* Oct. 1935.

9. Janet Flanner, *Paris Was Yesterday, 1925–1938* (New York: Viking Press, 1972).

10. Eric Corder, *Murder, My Love: The Great Crimes of Passion* (Chicago: Playboy Press, 1974).

BLANCA DE SAULLES

1. Evans, *The Valentino Affair.*
2. Natacha Rambova, *Rudolph Valentino: A Wife's Memories of an Icon* (Hollywood, CA: PVG Pub., 2009).
3. Evans, *The Valentino Affair.*

PAULINE DUBUISSON

1. Derick Goodman, *Crime of Passion* (London: Elek Books, 1958).
2. Albert Borowitz, *Blood and Ink: An International Guide to Fact-Based Crime Literature* (Kent, OH: Kent State Univ. Press, 2002).

PRINCESS FAHMY

1. Edward Grice, *Great Cases of Sir Henry Curtis Bennett K.C.* (London: Hutchinson, 1937).
2. French: a prostitute, or a kept woman.
3. Andrew Rose, *The Woman before Wallis: Prince Edward, the Parisian Courtesan, and the Perfect Murder* (New York: Picador, 2013).
4. Lucy Bland, *Modern Women on Trial: Sexual Transgression in the Age of the Flapper* (Manchester: Manchester Univ. Press, 2013).

LAURA FAIR

1. Laura D. Fair, Andrew J. Marsh, and Samuel Osbourne, *Official Report of the Trial of Laura D. Fair: For the Murder of Alex. P. Crittenden, Including the Testimony, the Arguments of Counsel, and the Charge of the Court, Reported Verbatim and the Entire Correspondence of the Parties, with Portraits of the Defendant and the Deceased* (San Francisco: San Francisco Co-operative Printing, 1871).
2. Carole Haber, *The Trials of Laura Fair: Sex, Murder, and Insanity in the Victorian West* (Chapel Hill: Univ. of North Carolina Press, 2015).
3. Suzann Ledbetter, *Shady Ladies: Nineteen Surprising and Rebellious American Women* (New York: Tom Doherty Associates, 2006).
4. Laura D. Fair, *Wolves in the Fold: A Lecture* (San Francisco: Laura D. Fair, 1873).

ANNIE GEORGE

1. John Stark Bellamy II, *A Woman Scorned: The Murder of George Saxton* (N.p.: Kindle, 2011).

CLARA SMITH HAMON

1. Elmer D. McInnes and Lauretta Ritchie-McInnes, *Bud Ballew: Legendary Oklahoma Lawman* (Helena, MT: Twodot, 2008).

2. David R. Stokes, *Jake & Clara: Scandal, Politics, Hollywood and Murder* (Fairfax, VA: Critical Mass Books, 2015).

3. W. E. Weathers, 1921.

4. Mark Lynn Anderson, "Tempting Fate: Clara Smith Hamon, or, The Secretary as Producer," in *Looking Past the Screen: Case Studies in American Film History and Method,* ed. Jon Lewis and Eric Loren Smoodin (Durham, NC: Duke Univ. Press, 2007), 117–50.

CLAUDINE LONGET

1. Jay Robert Nash, *Murder among the Rich and Famous: Celebrity Slayings That Shocked America* (New York: Arlington House, 1987).

NELLIE MAY MADISON

1. Kathleen A. Cairns, *The Enigma Woman: The Death Sentence of Nellie May Madison* (Lincoln: Univ. of Nebraska Press, 2007).

JULIA MORRISON

1. Keven McQueen, *The Axman Came from Hell and Other Southern True Crime Stories* (Gretna, LA: Pelican Pub. Co., 2011).

CHARLOTTE NASH NIXON-NIRDLINGER

1. Mary Knight, *On My Own* (New York: Macmillan Co., 1938).

MADALYNNE OBENCHAIN

1. Craig Rice, ed. *Los Angeles Murders* (New York: Duell, Sloan & Pearce, 1947).

2. George Towne, "The Unsolved Murder in Beverly Glen," *Real Detective* 32, no. 1.

3. French: search for the woman. This phrase, coined by Alexandre Dumas, embodies the concept that for every riddle of human conduct, a woman features in the answer.

4. "Mrs. Obenchain, Burch Indicted in Murder Case," *New York Tribune,* Aug. 12, 1921.

5. Theodore Dreiser was fascinated by the psychology of attraction between an accused and an accuser. He once sought everything he could find concerning Madalynne Obenchain "and everything that relates to the District attorney—

Woolwine, who was the prosecutor, I don't know if it appeared in the papers there or not, but I heard from newspaper men that . . . when Woolwine was getting ready to prosecute her, he fell in love with her while she was in jail." Theodore Dreiser and Donald Pizer, *A Picture and a Criticism of Life* (Urbana: Univ. of Illinois Press, 2008).

6. Bakken, *Women Who Kill Men.*

BEATRICE PACE

1. Wood, *The Most Remarkable Woman in England.*

2. Wood, *The Most Remarkable Woman in England.*

GERTRUDE GIBSON PATTERSON

1. Sheila O'Hare and Alphild Dick, *Wicked Denver: Mile-High Misdeeds and Malfeasance* (Charleston, SC: History Press, 2012). For more in fiction, see Robert M. Hardaway, *Alienation of Affection: Based on the True Story of the Sensational 1911 Murder at Denver's Richthofen Castle* (Montrose, CO: Western Reflections Pub. Co., 2003).

2. Evans, *The Valentino Affair.*

NAN PATTERSON

1. Newman Levy, *The Nan Patterson Case* (New York: Simon and Schuster, 1959).

ALMA RATTENBURY

1. F. Tennyson Jesse, ed., *Trial of Alma Victoria Rattenbury and George Percy Stoner* (London: William Hodge & Co., 1935).

DAISY ROOT

1. Teresa R. Simpson, *Memphis: Murder & Mayhem* (Charleston, SC: History Press, 2008).

ABE SADA

1. German: sexually motivated murderer.

2. William Johnston, *Geisha, Harlot, Strangler, Star: A Woman, Sex and Morality in Modern Japan* (New York: Columbia Univ. Press, 2005). In film: *In the Realm of the Senses* (1976).

3. Lorena Bobbitt's case arose in 1993, when Lorena severed her husband's penis while he slept, earning headlines such as THE MANASSAS MUTILATION.

At trial, she claimed her act was prompted by temporary insanity after her husband raped her. She was acquitted. See Dershowitz, *The Abuse Excuse*.

MADELINE SMITH

1. Jessie McLachlan was accused of the murder of her friend. Tried in Glasgow in 1862, she was convicted and sentenced to hang. Public outcry led to a commutation of her sentence, and she served fifteen years in prison for her crime. See Christiana Brand, *Heaven Knows Who* (New York: Scribner, 1960).

2. The long, hard death of Charles Bravo by antimony poisoning has long been "the prize puzzle of British criminal jurisprudence." William Roughead, *Classic Crimes* (New York: New York Review; London: Bloomsbury, 2001). Many have taken a crack at solving the "whodunit" in the decades since Bravo was poisoned in 1876 and have given up in defeat, notably mystery author Agatha Christie (*Ordeal by Innocence* [New York: Harper, 2017]) and filmmaker Julian Fellowes (Julian Fellowes et al., *Julian Fellowes Investigates: A Most Mysterious Murder* [Hilversum: Just Bridge, 2011]). The murder victim, a bullish lawyer named Charles Bravo, was by every account—certainly that given by his young and beautiful wife of four months, Florence Bravo—cruel; he demanded his wife fulfill her sexual duties and indulge his proclivities even after she suffered a series of miscarriages. But there was a lover in the picture as well. Before their marriage (and, per her husband's suspicions, after their marriage as well), young Florence carried on an affair with a famous doctor almost three times her age. Add a wrongfully discharged stableman and a hostile housekeeper, and you have all the stock characters of a classic Christie plot. Bravo was dosed with a derivative of antimony—an exceptionally horrible poison to use for the purpose—and his excruciating death took three days. Someone must have hated him. He seemed befuddled by his illness and could not offer any plausible theories as to who may have poisoned him (Edmund L. Pearson, *More Studies in Murder* [London: Arco Pub., 1953]). The inquest that followed was so scandalous that women and children were banned from the room while Mrs. Bravo testified. But the journalists listened eagerly, and their reports were a worldwide sensation. Florence was forced to relay the shocking details of her affair with the doctor, and the inquisitors forced from her "shame-blanched lips" all the excruciating details of her sex life with her obnoxious mate down to her "toilet secrets," such as the color of her maidenhair (James Ruddick and Alastair Petrie, *Death at the Priory: Love, Sex, and Murder in Victorian England* [New York: Atlantic Monthly Press, 2002]). Despite the ridiculously punitive questioning, nothing was proven against Florence, or any other suspect. Nobody was ever arrested or charged, but they all lived under clouds of suspicion all their lives, particularly the attractive widow, who still keeps us guessing—did she or didn't she? (Mary S. Hartman, *Victorian Murderesses: A True History of Thirteen Respectable French and English Women Accused of Unspeakable Crimes* [Mineola, NY: Dover Publications, 2014]).

3. Florence Maybrick was an American who was convicted in Liverpool,

England, of poisoning her husband with arsenic in 1889. She was incarcerated for fourteen years. See Richard Jay Hutto, *A Poisoned Life: Florence Chandler Maybrick, the First American Woman Sentenced to Death in England* (Jefferson, NC: McFarland & Co., 2018).

4. Margaret Nicholas, *The World's Wickedest Women* (New York: Berkley Books, 1988).

5. H. M. Walbrook, *Murders and Murder Trials 1812–1912* (London: Constable, 1932).

6. Roughead, *Classic Crimes.*

7. Eleanor Gordon and Gwyneth Nair, *Murder and Morality in Victorian Britain: The Story of Madeleine Smith* (Manchester, UK: Manchester Univ. Press, 2009).

MARGUERITE STEINHEIL

1. Rose, *The Woman before Wallis.*

VERA STRETZ

1. Reynolds, *The Story of Samuel S. Leibowitz.*

2. Edward W. Knappman, Stephen G. Christianson, and Lisa Paddock, eds., *Great American Trials* (Farmington Hills, MI: Gale Group, 2002).

3. Colin Evans, *Blood on the Table: The Greatest Cases of New York City's Office of the Chief Medical Examiner* (New York: Berkeley Books, 2008).

4. Franklin Jonas and Diana Klebanow, *People's Lawyers: Crusaders for Justice in American History* (Armonk, NY: M. E. Sharpe, 2002).

5. Harold Schechter, *The Mad Sculptor: The Maniac, the Model, and the Murder That Shook a Nation* (Boston: New Harvest, 2014).

COUNTESS MARIE O'ROURKE TARNOVSKA

This chapter originally appeared as "The World's Worst Woman" in *Masters of True Crime: Chilling Stories of Murder and the Macabre,* ed. R. Barri Flowers (Amherst, NY: Prometheus Books, 2012), and is reprinted with the permission of the publisher.

1. Anna Mary Babey, *Americans in Russia, 1776–1917* (New York: Comet Press, 1938).

2. Charles Boswell and Lewis Thompson, *Advocates of Murder* (New York: Collier Books, 1962).

3. Private interview with Tatjana Hine (Tarnovska), Chicago, June 2009.

4. Elliott O'Donnell, *Fatal Kisses, in History and Tradition* (London: John Hamilton Ltd., 1929).

5. Claudio Dell'Orso and Andrea Salmaso, *L'Affare de Russi* (ebook), http://www.hotelala.it/img/libro_contessa.pdf.

6. Catherine Lingua, *Ces anges du bizarre* (Paris: Libr. Nizet, 1995).

7. Brad Steiger, *Bizarre Beauties* (Chicago: Camerarts, 1965).

EPILOGUE

1. Pulitzer, *A Woman Scorned.*

2. Robert J. MacCoun, "The Emergence of Extralegal Bias during Jury Deliberation," *Criminal Justice and Behavior* 17 (1990): 303.

2/20